Introduction

In 1917, the distinguished British theologian Peter Taylor Forsyth wrote that "the ecclesiastical question of the hour is not that of the laity (as at the Reformation) but that of the ministry."[1] Forsyth meant that the most pressing issue facing ecclesiology, the theology of the church, had to do with the life and work of the clergy. It is a matter of emphasis, of course. The church's ministry always includes both clergy and laity; but I think the ecclesiastical question of the hour in the late-twentieth century is again the nature and purpose of ordained ministry. This book is an effort to understand the history and theology of ordination in Methodism. It grew out of an interest sparked by my involvement in the training of persons for the future ministry of the church, my service on a Board of Ordained Ministry, and my research and teaching in ecclesiology.

The initial development of these ideas was for the Franklin S. Hickman Lectures at Duke University, which I delivered in the Fall of 1985. Dr. Hickman served on the faculty of Duke Divinity School from 1927 to 1953 as Professor of Psychology of Religion and of Preaching. He was also Preacher to the University. The Hickman Lectures were endowed with a generous gift from his widow, Mrs. Vera Hickman, in 1966. I am grateful to the committee which invited me to give the lectures, because it provided the stimulus and required me to take the time to organize my thinking and do the writing.

7

INTRODUCTION

I am indebted to many persons who have heard me lecture on this subject at several universities, seminaries, and pastors' schools, and have offered helpful counsel.

I am particularly thankful to my students and colleagues at Duke Divinity School, and my colleagues in the ordained ministry, who have helped to shape and sharpen my thinking. My secretary, Lois Blanton, has given many hours to this manuscript; and my family, Leesa, Margaret and Trevor, have contributed the interest and support without which I could not have finished.

Contents

the Yoke of
OBEDIENCE

"We take upon ourselves with joy the yoke of obedience, ... We are no longer our own, but thine."

- John Wesley, *The Covenant Service*

the Yoke of
OBEDIENCE

The Meaning of Ordination in Methodism

Dennis M. Campbell

Abingdon Press / Nashville

THE YOKE OF OBEDIENCE
The Meaning of Ordination in Methodism

Copyright © 1988 by Abingdon Press

ISBN 0-687-46660-1

Scripture quotations are from the Revised Standard Version of
the Bible, copyright 1946, 1952, 1971 by the Division of
Christian Education of the National Council of the Churches of
Christ in the USA. Used by permission.

MANUFACTURED BY THE PARTHENON PRESS AT
NASHVILLE, TENNESSEE, UNITED STATES OF AMERICA

Chapter I
The Nature of the Question

Hence I remind you to rekindle the gift of God that is within you
through the laying on of my hands . . . .

– 1 Timothy 1:6

Ordination has not been a major issue for most Methodists.
Lay persons have generally thought of it, if at all, as authorizing, or credentialing, of persons to "work as ministers." Clergy
have viewed it as a step in the complex process leading to
service as a pastor. It has been seen as the public-worship side
of official acceptance into the annual conference, which takes
place at an executive session of clergy members of the
conference. The real issue for Methodists has been annual
conference membership, which admits one to itinerant ministry in the connection, and which is prior to ordination as an
elder.

The lack of attention to ordination was made clear to me
once when, as a member of the Board of Ordained Ministry, I
asked a candidate for Elder's Orders to explain theologically
what would happen in the ordination service when the bishop
placed hands on the ordinand's head. The young man was
unable to answer the question, except to say that he would then
have the credentials to be a minister. I asked him why we didn't
just mail the certificate of credentials and save the annual
conference the expense and time of an ordination service? He
could not give a good reason. He is not alone. I realized then

that many students never deal specifically with the theology of ordination in seminary.

In the history of Methodism the subject ordinarily has arisen only in regard to the question of the legitimacy of Wesley's ordinations, or the relationship between ordination and sacramental ministry. American episcopal Methodists early satisfied themselves about the legitimacy of their orders, especially as a result of Bishop Asbury's articulation of the matter. The dominant Methodist bodies (including those in the Evangelical United Brethren traditions) never deviated from the view that ordination is required for the administration of the sacramental ministries of Baptism and the Lord's Supper (though exceptions have been made to accommodate the pastoral needs of charges served by local pastors under appointment). But on the whole Methodists were too pragmatic to worry about the fine points of the theology of ordination. They were inclined to find the legitimacy and authenticity of ministry in the results of the preachers' work for church and society. Recently, however, ordination has become a major issue for both clergy and laity in United Methodism and in other Christian churches as well.

The Urgency of the Topic for the Whole Church

There are a number of reasons why ordination is so current a topic.

1. *We are struggling to understand more fully the meaning of ministry.* A growing emphasis on the ministry of the whole church, both laity and clergy, has resulted in new attention to the role of all Christians as ministers. This has challenged the popular view that ordained ministers are "hired to do the work of the church." It has also reminded the laity of their obligations for the church's ministry. Ministry is the work of the whole church. It takes place not only in the buildings in which the church meets, and not only within the Christian community, but also in the larger communities of the world we all inhabit. The way in which Christian ministry happens in the world is not easy to work out, and is never fully understood.

THE NATURE OF THE QUESTION

One of the great needs in contemporary Christianity is better articulation of, and reflection about, the ministry of Christ's people in the world.

There is an essential place for ordination in the ministry of all believers, but the meaning of ordination, and the exact purpose of a "set apart" ministry, needs precise definition in the context of the wholeness of Christian ministry. How exactly do self-denial, commitment, obedience and service get translated into reality in professional ministry? The relationship between lay and ordained ministries, and the function of each, needs to be understood so that all the varieties of gifts given by God to the church can be used and mutually appreciated.

2. *We are struggling with the relationship between renewal in ministry and renewal in the church.* United Methodism is undergoing a great deal of self-analysis in the light of membership decline. But concern about the vitality of the church has to do with more than membership. There are issues of identity, spiritual life, commitment, and service which worry sensitive commentators. A great deal of attention is being given to the ordained ministry because the health of any church is related to the quality of its leadership. I often have lay persons ask me why we cannot produce more excellent clergy. The supposition is that only significant renewal of the ordained ministry will assure the future of the church.

Renewal in ministry involves both lay and clergy; and both are essential for the future. The history of Christianity shows, however, that there is a specific need for excellence in ordained ministerial leadership if the church is to be effective. Exactly how renewal comes to the ordained ministry is complex theologically because there are both divine and human dimensions. Academic excellence and training in skill development are not enough. The real issue is spiritual. Unless ordained ministers are spiritually alive they are no good. We cannot control God's provision of leadership for the church, but we can be certain that the human dimension is responsive to the needs of the church and do everything possible to work actively for renewal in the ranks of the ordained.

THE NATURE OF THE QUESTION

3. *We are struggling to understand how God's call and the call of the church work together to provide an adequate supply of ordained ministers for the church.* There is evidence that the coming decade will see a striking decline in the number of ordained ministers available for appointment to congregations. A number of factors are involved including a large number of retirements of clergy who came into the ministry in the 1950's, an increase in early retirements, and the departure of some clergy in middle age for other vocations. Also, the average age of seminarians has risen since the early 1970's. Now many seminarians are second-career persons who will have relatively short tenures in the ministry. The old pattern where one would go into ministry and serve for forty years or more is less prevalent. In the last ten years there has been a dramatic increase in the number of women in seminary. Now thirty-five percent of Protestant seminarians are female, and in some United Methodist seminaries women constitute fifty percent of the student body. It is still too early to judge what the long-term pattern of women in ministry will be, however. Women, especially, have tended to be older while in seminary, and there is some evidence that the number of second-career women coming into the seminaries has leveled off.

United Methodism is receiving its clergy in increasing numbers from other denominations. This means persons come into Methodism when they enter ministry, even though they have not grown up in the denomination. Our system of guaranteed appointments is especially attractive to persons who come out of churches with congregational polities, and our theological openness attracts many.[1]

We have also experienced a period in American society when the service occupations have been popularly out of favor. The ministry, education, the professoriate and social work have not had as many applicants as medicine, law and business.[2] Obviously the ministry is significantly different from other occupations. The way we judge quality and success is also complex, because the ministry of the church requires a wide variety of persons and skills.

All of these factors have contributed to a situation in which I think United Methodism will experience a shortage of ordained ministers before long. We cannot recruit for ministry as if it were simply one among numerous vocations. Nevertheless, we need to give increased attention to the way in which we can help persons recognize God's call to ministry and prepare for ordained leadership in the church.

4. *We are struggling to understand and articulate standards and qualifications for ordination.* The ministry of the Christian church always has been shaped by the culture it has served even as it has shaped culture. This is obviously true of the Methodist ministry in America. In the last twenty years Methodism's ordained ministry has undergone some major changes. Increased educational requirements have made seminary the norm, and continuing education mandatory. More regular and organized evaluation procedures include lay participation in addition to the district superintendent and bishop. Women constitute a growing percentage of the clergy. We have a significant number of clergy couples and growing numbers of clergy whose spouses have their own professional careers. The ordained ministry has not escaped the societal reality of divorce, and while once divorce disqualified clergy, it is now not uncommon to find divorced persons serving as pastors.

There is tension in the church regarding ethical standards expected of ordained ministers. Traditional Methodist teachings regarding such matters of personal morality as the use of tobacco and beverage alcohol have undergone change. While once Methodist ministers took vows pledging not to smoke or drink, the 1968 *Book of Discipline* removed the specific prohibitions and imposed what the General Conference called "higher standards of self-discipline and habit formation in all personal and social relationships."[3] This required a minister to examine all aspects of his or her behavior. Many in the church do not look with favor on ministers interpreting this to mean that they may choose to use tobacco or alcohol, even if they claim to do so responsibly. Others welcome the recognition on the part of the church that moral issues go beyond such matters of

13

personal morality. The way in which ordained ministers express their sexuality has also become a source of debate. Issues of clergy marriage, divorce and homosexuality are controversial, and especially so when discussed in the context of ordination. There is an urgent need for a higher level of debate on these issues of standards and qualifications which can only be realized through an understanding of the meaning of ordination.

5. *We are struggling to deal with the nature of theological education for ordained ministry.* Early Methodism was skeptical of formal education for ministry. Wesley himself broke with Oxford and insisted that the first qualification for ministry was not academic preparation, but the experience of a direct call from God. Wesley was an intellectual who appreciated education, however, and prescribed a formidable course of study for his preachers.[4] A major idea in Wesleyan theology is that knowledge and vital piety must be joined: "Unite the pair so long disjoined, Knowledge and vital piety."[5] In the rough conditions of the American frontier, knowledge was sometimes replaced by an ignorant piety. Wesley's effort to maintain a balance between education and faith by asserting the need for religious experience opened the door to irresponsible celebration of ignorance in the name of experiential religion. The widespread anti-intellectualism so characteristic of American society in the nineteenth century is especially evident in the fear that an educated ministry would threaten the church and the faith.

Nevertheless, by 1816, American Methodism instituted a Course of Study required of all candidates and supervised by the presiding elders.[6] In 1834, the Reverend John P. Durbin wrote a famous editorial in the *Christian Advocate* entitled "An Educated Ministry Among Us." Durbin advocated better education for all church members, and the idea was that by educating its members, the church would be educating its future clergy. Gradually advocates of seminary education arose. The earliest Methodist seminary opened in Concord, New Hampshire in 1847, and others followed.

14

Seminary education, however, was the exception rather than the rule for most Methodist ministers throughout the nineteenth century and half of the twentieth. All, even seminary graduates, were required to pass the Course of Study in order to be admitted to the annual conference. Only in more recent years have annual conferences increasingly required a seminary degree for full membership and exempted theological school graduates from the Course of Study. This step, by the way, has actually caused United Methodism to lose direct control of the education of its ministry. Under the Course of Study plan all ministers read the same books and therefore shared at least a common core of biblical, historical and theological literature.[7] Now United Methodist ministers are educated at a wide variety of seminaries, and there is no common core of education. Moreover, because of Methodist openness to diverse traditions, and for reasons of economics, demographics, and the supply of pastors for student charges, there has never been an attempt to require that Methodist pastors be educated in Methodist seminaries. We are one of the few major churches which does not now require its candidates for ordination to be educated in seminaries related to its own tradition. Almost half of current Methodist ministerial candidates are in non-United Methodist schools. This diversity can be very healthy; it can also be problematic for the long-range good of the church, especially if basic education in Wesleyan theology and Methodist polity is weak.

Virtually everyone has an opinion about the proper elements of an education for ministry, and the extent to which the church should control education for ordination is a question of immense importance and current debate. The question cannot be dealt with adequately, let alone answered, unless careful attention is given to the meaning of ordination.

6. *We are struggling to deal with ordination in an ecumenical context.* United Methodism is by no means alone in its attention to ordination. These questions are arising in most of the Protestant churches and in Roman Catholicism as well. Presbyterians and Lutherans in the United States have just undergone

church mergers necessitating extensive study of ministry and ordination. Lutheran introduction of a form of episcopacy has not been without tension.[8] The Episcopal Church, and the world-wide Anglican communion, are examining the theology of ordination as they deal with lay ministry, the diaconate, and especially the consecration of women as bishops.[9] Due to a number of social and cultural issues, including a dramatic decline in North America of candidates for ordination, the Roman Catholic Church is being challenged from within to examine its own history and theology of ministry.[10] All of these churches, and others as well, are engaged in a variety of international bi-lateral and multi-lateral dialogues on matters of ministry and ordination.

The Consultation on Church Union, in the United States, and the World Council of Churches both have produced significant documents concerning ministry. In particular, the Lima Document of the World Council's Faith and Order Commission, *Baptism, Eucharist, and Ministry*, evidences remarkable ecumenical convergence.[11]

United Methodism, as a branch on the trunk of the Christian tradition, and as a part of the worldwide church of Jesus Christ, deals with the meaning of ministry and ordination in an ecumenical context. Methodism has a rich and evolving tradition which shapes our understanding of the meaning of ordination. Continuing research and reflection is helping us to learn more about our own heritage as we seek to interpret that heritage responsibly in a time of ecumenical development and promise.

To Inform and To Renew

The purpose of this book is to inform and to renew the ministry of the whole people of God. The questions arising as a result of the complex factors noted above deserve thoughtful attention. All members of the church need to consider the nature and purpose of ordination. To accomplish that consideration requires, in the first place, biblical and historical study. One cannot deal with, let alone understand, the meaning of ordination in Methodism unless one knows something about its biblical and historical roots. Accordingly we will look first at the ministry of the church with reference to the Bible and the history of ecumenical Christianity.

Ministry and ordination also have a specific tradition within Methodism. While he never developed a systematic theology of ministry, Wesley wrote extensively on the subject and instituted a structure of ministry which has informed Methodism ever since. American episcopal Methodism also was shaped by the uniqueness of the American experience, and we will give attention to the way in which Methodist ministry both influenced and was influenced by its culture. Examination of ordination cannot be only historical however. The ministry of the church is not static, and systematic theological reflection is required to understand the representative character of ordained ministers and the meaning of ordination in our time.

This book is not an attempt to propose new ordering of Methodist ministry. For several quadrennia commissions have been studying ministry in United Methodism. Their reports have occasioned sometimes heated debate, usually about the role of lay professional ministries and the nature of the diaconate. At heart the issues have been related to identity and placement in the annual conference. These discussions have required new reflection about itineracy, appointment, and the essential character of Methodist ministry. I hope this book will illuminate those discussions, without entering them directly, through the presentation of what has been, and is currently, the church's teaching about ministry.

It is urgent that the whole church understand something of the history and theology of ordination so that the pressing issues facing us can be dealt with from an informed position. In the final analysis, ministry is not a matter of structure and organization, but of theology and mission. Authenticity in the church's ministry requires us to give priority to theology. Theology is certainly related to sociology, economics, politics and all other aspects of human experience, but theology must never be reduced to such realities.

There is a certain cynicism about ordained ministry abroad in the church today. On the part of the laity this is suggested by the suspicion that concerns for benefits and promotion have supplanted obedience and service on the part of some clergy. The anti-clericalism this attitude can foster spells death to the church for numerous reasons which will be made clear later. On the part of clergy it takes the form of acquiescence in a system that can be used for self-interest and self-promotion. The triumph of obsession with career advancement and political process gives sad evidence to this reality. It is essential for the present state and future shape of the church that such cynicism be overcome. I think it can be overcome only by the renewal, through God's grace, of our understanding of the meaning of ministry, and our faithful commitment to act accordingly.

The purpose of this book, then, is not only to inform, but also to invite us all, lay and clergy alike, to renewal in our ministries. Particularly, of course, I hope that men and women called by God and the church to ordained ministry will find this book an occasion for reaffirmation of call and vows. The words of 2 Timothy 1:6 are appropriate: "Hence I remind you to rekindle the gift of God that is within you through the laying on of my hands . . . ."

My text and theme come from John Wesley's Covenant Service:

"We take upon ourselves with joy the yoke of obedience, . . . We are no longer our own but thine."

The question facing ministry today is whether we will let that prayer be our own; whether we will "bind ourselves with willing bonds to our covenant God, and take the Yoke of Christ upon us."[12]

Chapter II
The Ministry of the Whole People of God

... that the congregation of the Lord may not be as sheep which have no shepherd.

–Numbers 27:17

All Christian believers are called to ministry. Sometimes this idea is not understood because of the tendency to use the term "ministry" to refer popularly to those who are engaged in full-time professional service in the church, usually ordained ministers. Thus we speak of one entering "the ministry" and we mean the occupation of the clergy, full-time ministry for pay, sociologically not unlike other classic professions of medicine and law, or other occupations by which men and women earn livings in our society. This narrow usage of the term ministry is unfortunate, however, because it seriously truncates the wider and richer understanding of Christian ministry in the Bible and church teaching.

The call to ministry is a basic idea in the life of the church. The Greek word from the New Testament is *diakonia*. Its meaning is service. To be a member of the community of those who follow Jesus is to be part of a community committed to service. Jesus called disciples to lives of obedience and service; and he commissioned them to gather others who would commit themselves to his idea and vision. Jesus proposed an inversion of the usual way in which women and men think about greatness and service. Greatness in the eyes of the world involves power, rights and privileges. According to Jesus, greatness has to do with the relinquishing of such human values and the commitment to service and sacrifice. Trying to explain this to his disciples, Jesus said, "You know that those who are supposed to rule over the Gentiles lord it over them, and their great men exercise authority over them. But it shall not be so among you; but whoever would be great among you must be your servant, and whoever would be first among you must be slave of all. For the Son of man also came not to be served but to serve, and to give his life as a ransom for many" (Mark 10:42-45). Jesus himself is thus the great exemplar of service. He gave his life that others might live. As the body of Jesus Christ in the world, the entirety of the church exists for service.

Entry into the church is therefore entry into ministry. Baptism, the sacrament by which persons are initiated into the Christian community, may be thought of as an admission to the general ministry of the church. The vows of Baptism, reaffirmed in Confirmation or other services of baptismal renewal, commit the Christian to a life of love and service in the world as a member of the body of Christ.

Ministry in the New Testament Church

The understanding that all Christian believers are called to be obedient to Christ in ministry of service comes from the New Testament. Any consideration of ministry, and the meaning of ordination, needs to begin with the New Testament and certainly ministry in the Wesleyan tradition, as will be made clear later, is understood to be scriptural. The New Testament demonstrates a variety of patterns of ministry in the early church. It is not surprising that this should be so. The early church was struggling to determine how best its mission could be carried out; there obviously was no Christian tradition, and so early Christians tried to remain faithful to Jesus, to learn from their Jewish heritage, and to borrow from secular experience as they sought to enact the ministry of the church. No one pattern is dominant in the New Testament, but certain theological conclusions can be drawn. It is important first to comprehend the basic patterns of ministry represented in the New Testament.

All Christian ministry derives from Jesus Christ and therefore we begin with the picture of ministry presented by the synoptic gospels of the earthly life of Jesus. Jesus was a reformer who provided an alternative approach within Judaism to the hereditary priesthood and conventional patterns of established religion. In the gospels, ministry is centered in Jesus. We refer to Jesus' ministry and we mean his whole life. Even so he gathers a group of followers and invites them, through example and teaching, to join him in ministry. His own ministry is unique, but his followers were to be what we would think of as a movement of lay persons called to lives of obedience and service. Jesus' followers constituted a kind of lay renewal movement within Judaism.[1] From the beginning, Jesus set aside some persons for particular leadership. His identification of the twelve disciples, "whom he named apostles," is the chief example of Jesus' intention to provide leadership for his movement.[2]

It is also clear that, from the beginning, the matter of leadership was problematic. Even the apostles misunderstood the nature of Jesus' servant character and their commission to be obedient servants as well. Among themselves they would argue about "place" and "priority" and Jesus would struggle to help them understand how they could be at once servants and leaders.[3] Never, however, did Jesus reject the need for leadership, and he recognized differences of leadership capability among the apostles. The tradition of Peter's priority, for instance, derives from the gospel account of his recognition of Jesus as "the Christ, the son of the living God."[4] This affirmation demonstrated his ability to articulate, through the grace of God, the truth of God in Christ, and thus to be capable of passing on the gospel message.

The gospels show Jesus as an intentional leader who gathered around himself a group who were also commissioned as leaders. The nature of this leadership was difficult for his followers to grasp because Jesus presented a new vision of a community of service led by persons who were themselves

21

servants of the servant community. This model was exemplified by Jesus himself who, "though he was in the form of God,
did not count equality with God a thing to be grasped, but
emptied himself, taking the form of a *servant*, being born in
human likeness. And being found in human form he *humbled*
himself and became *obedient* unto death, even death on a cross
(Phil. 2:6-8, emphasis is mine).

After the Resurrection, and the gift of the Holy Spirit to the
church, earliest Christianity manifested several patterns of
ministry which, while different from one another, were consistent with the picture the gospels present of Jesus, and were
appropriate at the time for the mission of the church. One of
these is portrayed by Paul in his first letter to the church at
Corinth, written from Ephesus about 54 A.D.[5] This is probably
the earliest writing in the New Testament from the Christian
community on the subject of ministry. The picture presented is
one of ministries which are functional and charismatic. In his
letter, Paul explains that not all Christian believers are the
same, but that all are given gifts, through the grace of God,
which contribute to the total ministry of the church:

> Now there are varieties of gifts, but the same Spirit; and there are
> varieties of service, but the same Lord; and there are varieties of
> working, but it is the same God who inspires them all in every-
> one. To each is given the manifestation of the Spirit for the com-
> mon good. To one is given, through the Spirit, the utterance of
> wisdom, to another the utterance of knowledge according to the
> same Spirit, to another faith by the same Spirit, to another gifts
> of healing by the one Spirit, to another the working of miracles,
> to another prophecy, to another the ability to distinguish
> between spirits, to another various kinds of tongues, to another
> the interpretation of tongues. All of these are inspired by one
> and the same Spirit, who apportions to each one individually as
> he wills.
>
> (1 Cor. 12:4-11)

Following this basic statement, Paul introduces his classic
description of the church as the body of Christ. As the body has
many parts, and the parts each have their purpose, so the

church is composed of many persons with multiple gifts. Not all are the same, yet they are given by God to work together for the common good:

> For just as the body is one and has many members, and all the members of the body, though many, are one body, so it is with Christ . . . . For the body does not consist of one member but of many . . . . As it is, there are many parts, yet one body . . . . Now you are the body of Christ and individually members of it.
>
> (1 Cor. 12:12,14,20,27)

There are numerous other places in Paul's writings where he expresses this view of the church as the body of Christ and the members of the body as ministers who have particular gifts to bring to the whole.[6] These writings suggest that in the earliest New Testament church there was a clear conviction that all followers of Jesus Christ are called to ministry, and that the total ministry of the church is made up of the contributions of the many and diverse gifts manifested in actual lives of service on the part of Christian believers. There are varieties of gifts given by God's providence to serve the church and build the body of Christ:

> And his gifts were that some should be apostles, some prophets, some evangelists, some pastors and teachers, for the equipment of the saints, for the work of ministry, for building up the body of Christ . . . .
>
> (Eph. 4:11-12)

In this pattern of ministry the various gifts for ministry are functional and charismatic. They were functional in that they made contributions toward specific needs of the whole community. They are charismatic in that they are given by God and recognized by the community because of their functional value, their contribution to the vitality of the total ministry, rather than because of an official position, special training or inherited status.[7]

The picture Paul presents of the Christian movement in its earliest manifestation after the earthly life of Jesus is thus one of continuity with what the gospels suggest to be the shape of the servant movement Jesus drew to himself. It is the picture of a community in which all followers of Christ are in ministry, in which there is recognized a variety of gifts, and in which these gifts are judged in regard to their contribution to the needs of the whole community. Although there is a fundamental equality among all Christian believers, some are given gifts for leadership within the community which sets them apart as servants of the servant community. This leadership, as Paul demonstrates it, is a leadership which includes responsibility for teaching authority so that the nature and purpose of the Christian community is consistent with the intentions of God as they were manifest in Jesus Christ.[8]

Another pattern of ministry in the earliest church was structured on the model of the synagogue. The separation between Christianity and Judaism was gradual and took many years. It was natural that Jewish followers of Jesus Christ would find the synagogue model appropriate for ministry.[9] Certain leaders in the church were recognized as "elders." This pattern did not contradict the charismatic pattern, because the basic theology of the variety of gifts could be comprehended within it, but it did involve an affirmation of "official" status accorded to some leaders. These leaders made decisions on behalf of the church and were shapers of teaching and mission. Thus from its earliest period the church recognized that some of its members needed to be given authority to act on behalf of the whole, particularly in matters of teaching. Luke, writing the story of the early church toward the end of the first century A.D., tells how the community was structured for worship, teaching and mission.[10] In the established Jewish-Christian communities, most notably in Jerusalem, the synagogue model prevailed, and these communities exercised authority for Christian practice. Even Paul came to Jerusalem to confer with "the apostles and the elders" about the mission to the Gentiles and to determine what would be required of Gentile converts.[11]

The early church ordered its life so that there would be leadership for the needs of Christians resident in communities and for evangelistic mission, particularly among the Gentiles.

Books from the later period of New Testament Christianity further elaborate models of ministry. The role of evangelists and teachers continued, as did the office of elder. In Titus 1:5-6, for instance, there is the directive to "appoint elders in every town. . . , men who are blameless, married only once, whose children are believers and not open to the charge of being profligate or insubordinate."

The Greek word for elder is *presbyteros*. They were leaders of the church who had particular responsibilities for specific congregations and provided ministry in congregations like what we think of as ordained ministry. Paul and Barnabas selected and appointed elders, and the tradition of elders being appointed by apostles, or disciples of apostles, continued into the late first century.[12] The role of the elder as one to whom a congregation is entrusted is demonstrated in 1 Peter 5:1-4:

> So I exhort the elders among you, as a fellow elder and a witness of the sufferings of Christ as well as a partaker in the glory that is to be revealed. Tend the flock of God that is your charge, not by constraint but willingly, not for shameful gain but eagerly, not as domineering over those in your charge but being examples to the flock. And when the chief shepherd is manifested you will obtain the unfading crown of glory.

Thus elders, or *presbyteroi*, were appointed to be shepherds to the flock of Christians in particular locations and they were to model themselves after Christ, the chief shepherd. Elders were to teach, care for the sick, order the life of the community, and be examples to the church.[13] The pattern of elders in ministry seems to have been normative especially among Christians closely related to the Jewish-Christian tradition whose experience with the synagogue model made it natural.[14]

In the Pastoral Epistles of Titus and Timothy there appear two other ministerial "offices," that of bishop (*episkopos*) and deacon (*diakonos*). *Episkopos* means overseer, or superintendent, and a *diakonos* is one who serves. In 1 Timothy 3 there is a statement of qualifications for the jobs of bishop and deacon:

THE MINISTRY OF THE WHOLE PEOPLE OF GOD

The saying is sure: If anyone aspires to the office of bishop, he desires a noble task. Now a bishop must be above reproach, the husband of one wife, temperate, sensible, dignified, hospitable, an apt teacher, no drunkard, not violent but gentle, not quarrelsome, and no lover of money. He must manage his own household well, keeping his children submissive and respectful in every way; for if a man does not know how to manage his own household, how can he care for God's church? He must not be a recent convert, or he may be puffed up with conceit and fall into the condemnation of the devil; moreover, he must be well thought of by outsiders, or he may fall into reproach and the snare of the devil.

Deacons likewise must be serious, not double-tongued, not addicted to much wine, not greedy for gain; they must hold the mystery of the faith with a clear conscience. And let them also be tested first; then if they prove themselves blameless let them serve as deacons.

(1 Tim. 3:1-10)

These two offices were related to one another; the deacon traditionally was an assistant to the bishop. The bishop in the early church was the pastoral leader of Christians in a particular community, a pastoral superintendent in a congregation.

We can see that by the end of the first century A.D., the New Testament church was setting forth specific characteristics which it sought in persons who would hold ministerial offices. The church specified certain qualifications for leadership in the community and asserted its right and responsibility to make judgments about the suitability of persons for leadership from its earliest period. The criteria indicate that the church had high standards for service in these offices and that it mattered a great deal how they were perceived not only within the community but also by those outside. Persons in these roles were to be "official" representatives of the church and, therefore, they had to be above reproach.

Bishops and deacons seem to be the pattern in Gentile Christianity, as elders were the pattern for church leadership in Jewish Christianity. The term and idea of *episkopos* derived from Roman civil authority. The church thus borrowed patterns of leadership which worked elsewhere, although it must not be thought that there was any exact system. The evidence is that there was much diversity, even to the extent that in some places the roles of elder (*presbyteros*) and bishop (*episkopos*) were one office. This is the case in Titus 1:5-9:

> This is why I left you in Crete, that you might amend what was defective, and appoint elders in every town as I directed you, men who are blameless, married only once, whose children are believers and not open to the charge of being profligate or insubordinate. For a bishop, as God's steward, must be blameless; he must not be arrogant or quick tempered or a drunkard or violent or greedy for gain, but hospitable, a lover of goodness, master of himself, upright, holy, and self-controlled; he must hold firm to the sure word as taught, so that he may be able to give instruction in sound doctrine and also to confute those who contradict it.

Here we see that the *presbyteros-episkopos* is to be blameless in character, a model to the church and the world, and a responsible teacher of the apostolic faith who can instruct with authority. The roles of elder and bishop are here merged into one office of leadership in the early church.

We have now examined the major expressions of ministry found in the New Testament. We have seen that in Jesus himself ministry was uniquely exemplified and that he gathered a community of followers who were to become obedient to his command that they, too, minister to the world. Jesus commissioned leaders for the community, though there was no "official" conception of leadership in the community until later. In the early post-Resurrection church leadership was both charismatic and structured. The charismatic ministries were gifts of the Holy Spirit given variously to members of the community for the good of the church. The structured ministries were primarily modeled after the synagogue with elders as the leaders. Later the "official" roles of bishop and deacon appeared. Bishop (*episkopos*) was a word and office used in Roman civil government and adopted by the church.[15]

27

The picture of ministry in the New Testament is one of great diversity. Multiple patterns are represented and no one pattern is normative.[16] Scholars agree that there is no model of ecclesiastical polity sanctioned in the canon.[17] Nevertheless certain generalizations about ministry in the New Testament can be made:

1. All Christians are called to ministry. Ministry is the vocation of all followers of Jesus Christ who rightly understand his call to obedience in service to the Christian community and the world.

2. There are varieties of gifts given by God through the Holy Spirit for the good of the whole church.

3. From the beginning the church recognized the need for some persons to be set apart for leadership of the community. These leaders were to articulate the gospel of Jesus Christ, to teach the faith, to help others practice the faith in daily life, and to be exemplars of the faith representing Christ to church and world.

4. There is no precise understanding of church polity in the New Testament. No specific ordering of the offices of elder, bishop and deacon is to be found, but they are scriptural and evidence the place of "official" roles of leadership in the church from its early days.

Ministry in the Early Church

We have seen that although leadership is clearly present, the New Testament provides no one conception of Christian ministry but several patterns. One gets no sense of formal organization of a "clergy" in the New Testament, no treatment of ordination or precise duties of church leaders.[18] It was the early church, following the period of New Testament Christianity, which further refined matters of leadership.

The need for organization was not apparent to the earliest Christians since it was supposed that Christ would soon return to redeem his people. As time went on, and as second generation Christians were present, it was necessary to attend to structure, organization and planning for the future. It is a sociological truism that human communities must be organized for effective existence. Leadership is necessary for organization to be effective. No human community can function devoid of leadership. Already in the New Testament we detect a gradual evolution from an emphasis on charismatic-functional ministries to "official" ministries with clearly-stated qualifications and objectives. Even if these "offices" were not structured or defined, they provided pastoral care for early residential communities of Christians.

In the second century, as the church expanded over a wide geographical area incorporating growing numbers of converts, most of whom were Gentiles unfamiliar with Christianity's Jewish roots, the need for leadership and the problem of unity became even more acute than it had been in the first century.[19] How was the church to work toward some unity of belief and practice in the face of rapid expansion and encounter with new cultures? This problem took two forms; on the one hand, the issue was unity of belief. This is the matter of teaching authority. In order that the basic affirmations of the gospel be communicated consistently, there needed to be assurance that certain persons were commissioned to proclaim the "right teaching" of the church. On the other hand, the issue was unity of moral practice. This has to do with right action, or the ethical implications of the gospel. It is essential to understand that right teaching and right practice go together. To understand the command of the gospel to radical obedience in the ministry of the church is to see a unity of faith and practice. There was no tradition of Christianity, and thus no precedent to which appeal could be made, and the early church began to experience dissension and disruption which threatened its unity and its effectiveness as a new movement.

To counter tendencies toward dissension and disruption in matters of teaching, the early church increasingly saw the necessity of having the "official" representatives of the community take responsibility for these matters. By the third century, teaching the Christian faith was entrusted to the "clergy," in an effort to assure its apostolic character.[20] The idea of a "clergy" arose in response to the need of the church for leadership in regard to right teaching. Already this concern was present in the New Testament, but it was exaggerated by the realities of rapid expansion.

The idea of a "clergy" (*kleros*) was first set forth by the priestly writers of the Old Testament.[21] In Numbers 11:16-17, 24-25 and 27:15-23 a distinction is made between the people and one set apart for the responsibility of leadership of the congregation:

> Let the Lord, the God of the spirits of all flesh, appoint a man over the congregation, who shall go out before them and come in before them, who shall lead them out and bring them in; that the congregation of the Lord may not be as sheep which have no shepherd.
>
> (Num. 27:16-17)

Ordination appears in the Old Testament in relationship to leadership of God's people. In Leviticus 8, the idea of "ordination" first emerges when Aaron and his sons are "consecrated" for service. We have seen how the New Testament church adopted the Jewish synagogue model of the council of elders for use in the Christian community. So too did the early church borrow the concept of a clergy and the ritual of ordination to appoint some to representative offices for the good of the whole.

Gradually there was an evolutionary merging of the systems of elders on the one hand, and bishops and deacons on the other within the concept of the clergy. This was a slow process which cannot be charted precisely. Irenaeus (d. 177 or 178), for instance, writes on teaching authority and uses *presbyteros* and *episkopos* interchangeably. Earlier in the second century, Ignatius of Antioch (d. 117) expressed a high view of the bishop when he wrote: be "obedient to the bishop, as Jesus Christ was to the Father. . . for where the bishop is, there is the catholic church."[22]   Bishops (or *presbyteroi-episkopoi*) functioned as pastors in local congregations, with deacons as their assistants. The term monarchical episcopacy refers to the institution of an episcopal office which worked toward unity in right teaching and right practice. The church was made complete by the bishop whose presence authorized official acts such as Holy Communion, Baptism, marriage, instruction or love feasts.[23]

The growth of the church resulted in need for superintendents over larger geographical areas. A pattern evolved in most areas in which the functions of *episkopos* and *presbyteros* were separated, with the bishop providing superintendence over multiple congregations and the elder becoming pastor in a local congregation. Elders exercised authority for presiding at the eucharist, for instruction and for other pastoral roles. The transition to greater clarity about clerical offices, functions and responsibilities took many years and was not uniform. Different Christian communities proceeded variously and regional patterns persisted for long periods.

The third century produced two important figures who greatly influenced the institutionalization of the clerical ministry. Hippolytus (d. 235 or 236) became a determinative shaper of liturgy as a result of his *Tradition Apostolica (Apostolic Tradition)*. While there are some evidences of the evolution of ordination in Christianity prior to the third century, Hippolytus offers the first major account of the practice and its rituals. His work includes rites for ordination of bishops, presbyters and deacons; and he restricts the term to those three ministries in his commentary on the meaning of the action. Cyprian (d. 258), the Bishop of Carthage, was a theorist of the nature and function of the ministry, and his treatise on the *Unity of the Catholic Church* is one of the most significant documents we possess about the church of the third century. Cyprian's articulation of a theology of ministry, and the liturgical ordering of Hippolytus, give witness to the fact that by the late third century a pattern of ordained ministry was largely in place.[24]

Bishops were understood as successors to the apostles. They were elected by local communities, from the elders, and Cyprian is explicit that the providential guidance of the Holy Spirit is active in the election. Because of this, bishops were to be obedient to the call to episcopacy even against their wills. Bishops often ended up as martyrs, and the office did not provide much worldly glory anyway, so men did not necessarily want it.[25] Bishops were ordained with the laying on of hands by other bishops (from other areas of the church) and presbyters, and through the prayer for the gift of the Holy Spirit.

Presbyters were likened to the elders of the Old Testament (Num. 11:17-25) and were linked with the bishops as members of the *kleros*. Although their functions were different, the exact distinction between the *presbyteros* and *episkopos* was not precise, and for this reason the ordination of the elder was done by the bishop and other elders. Deacons, on the other hand, were of a different order (not members of the *kleros*) and they remained tied to the bishop. Their functions were determined by the bishop, and he alone laid on hands in ordination.

Ordination signified authorization of persons called by God and commissioned by the church for responsibility for the faith. Ordination had to do chiefly with authenticity in assuring the apostolic character of Christian faith. This is why the idea of apostolic succession was so important. Bishops were identified as successors of the apostles because they were charged to maintain continuity with the message of Jesus and the faith of the earliest church. The bishop's role was especially that of teacher of the church in succession to the apostles.[26] The reason for reserving the presidential role at the Eucharist for the bishop, or the elder, was that the Eucharist brought together the essential elements of Christian teaching and practice. It was in the eucharistic celebration that the proclamation of the work, person and promise of Jesus Christ was most concretely evident. It was essential that these "holy mysteries" be administered by one who was "under orders," and "officially" obedient to the community, so that the people could be certain that they were served by a faithful shepherd.

Ordained ministers were examples to the church and to the world. Because of this, the early church continued the practice, noted in the Pastoral Epistles, of establishing high moral expectations for the clergy. Clergy represented the young church in a pagan world. They were the most visible Christians and it was essential that they be persons of whom the church could be proud. It was they who were most likely to undergo persecution for the faith and they had to be good models of martyrdom. As the idea of ordained ministerial orders developed, the expectation was that only persons of unblemished character should be ordained. Every effort was taken to prevent the possibility that one of its "representative" figures would cause the church embarrassment.

We have seen that it was in the post-New Testament period that ordained ministry developed as a part of the institutionalization of the church. This gradual development is difficult to trace because the history is not well documented and because the patterns were very diverse. Although specific practices and models varied among early Christian church communities, it is possible to make certain historical and theological generalizations:

1. *In the second and third centuries the early church continued the institutionalization we saw beginning in the New Testament.* This institutionalization was recognized as the work of the Holy Spirit to assure that the church, which, as the body of Christ in the world, is both divine and human, would be effective as a human community. In order to maintain continuity with the apostolic message, and to provide for unity as it grew rapidly, the church recognized a need for common teaching in regard to faith and practice.

2. *The idea of "clergy," persons set apart to be leaders and to be responsible for authorized teaching, was increasingly prevalent.* This concept was consistent with the Old Testament tradition of setting some apart for leadership. Further development of the New Testament ministerial offices of elders, bishops and deacons followed. Gradually patterns of relationship among the three offices came into place as did understandings of their responsibility for teaching, for liturgical leadership, and for ordering the life of the church.

3. *The practice of ordination, derived from Jewish tradition, developed to designate the setting apart of representative "officials" of the church for service as deacons, elders and bishops.* Ordination involved relinquishing the self, taking the yoke of obedience, and accepting possible martyrdom for the sake of the gospel and the life of the church of Jesus Christ.

4. *The church continued, expanded and elaborated the New Testament tradition of establishing criteria by which a person's adequacy for ministerial office was judged.* These qualifications included strict judgments about moral character since ordained ministers were "official" representative figures of Christ to the church and of the church to the world.

Ministry in Christian History

While Methodist understanding of ministry and ordination is shaped by the Bible and by the early church, developments in the conception of ministry in subsequent history also affected Wesley's views. While a full history is impossible in this book, some notice of major ideas and practices in the years between the early church and the emergence of Methodism in the eighteenth century is necessary if we are to understand Methodism's place in the larger tradition.[27]

A decisive change in the role and perception of ordained ministry came about as the result of the Emperor Constantine's conversion to Christianity in 312 A.D. Christianity was no longer regarded as a threat to the state, and ordained ministry was freed from the prospect of martyrdom and ignominy. This changed the character of the vocation, as did the subsequent establishment of Christianity as the official religion of the Roman Empire. The idea of a "career" in the church was borrowed from the state. The notion of hierarchy and a "ladder system," in which one progressively advances from the "bottom" to the "top," came from the Roman civil service and is not a new idea. It was in this period that the roles of deacon, presbyter and bishop were further defined and established in a hierarchical relationship to one another to adapt the official ministries of the church to a career model which provided both structure and a pattern of advancement. Thus ordinands began in the diaconate, progressed to the presbyterate and, for some, there was advancement to the episcopate. By the end of the fourth century the three orders, and their hierarchical relationship to one another, were recognized throughout the church.

The "career in ministry" pattern exaggerated the distinction between laity and clergy which developed in the early church. This distinction was increasingly clear as education became a hallmark of the clergy. Clergy were often the only persons systematically trained in even rudimentary skills of communication. Advanced learning became the province of the church, clergy were able to offer leadership for the culture because they were the only ones equipped to do so. The relationship between the clergy and education is therefore very old.

The medieval church carried the idea of the clergy as dominant leaders in the society to perhaps its greatest point in the history of the West. The three-fold order of deacon, presbyter and bishop was elaborated to include multiple minor lay and clerical orders and numerous superior levels of service. Medieval Europe was a "Christian culture" in which the church defined reality. Accordingly, the clergy occupied influential and powerful roles not limited to ecclesiastical affairs but including service in all arenas of society, even the highest levels of government. The religious orders (such as the Benedictines, Augustinians, Cistercians, Dominicans, and Franciscans) became great international institutions providing leadership for service, education, art and general culture. The combination of the clergy's virtual monopoly on education, the power of the orders, the economic strength of the church, and the support of the rulers resulted in the earliest university foundations.

Universities, in their early days, were church institutions whose professors were clergymen and whose scholars held at least minor clerical orders. The learned professions such as law and medicine became disciplines when clergy, committed to the ideal of service to individuals and to society, formed specialized faculties in the university to prepare persons for such vocations. The professions are rooted in the Christian theological idea of sacrifice and service; they began as specialized occupations of "religious professionals," persons who "professed" Christianity and whose commitment was to Christian service. Gradually the assumption that clerical orders were necessary for the professions began to change and laymen filled these roles, although university faculties were predominantly clergy for centuries.[28] One cannot understand John Wesley's Oxford unless one is aware of the continuing role of the church in education.

The picture of medieval culture is one in which the Christian view of reality was dominant and Christian institutions were pre-eminent. The central role of the church meant that the clergy had considerable power and authority. This power and authority came not only from political and economic strength, but also, and perhaps most importantly, from the idea of the sacramental power of the priesthood. Thomas Aquinas (1225-74) provided a brilliant philosophical summary of the theology of ordained ministry which had been growing in the Western Church for generations. His systematic articulation of the qualifications for, impediments to, and meaning of ordination established the view that presbyteral ordination (priestly orders, the word priest derives from *presbyteros*) results in a permanent, indelible character change, and was therefore a sacrament. The sacrament of ordination gave the priest power to grant or refuse forgiveness, as well as to perform the other sacramental ministries. Because this power was a permanent reality, ordained priesthood was regarded as a "state of life," and a priest's jurisdiction was not limited to a particular parish or community of believers. This came to be known as *ordinatio absoluta* (absolute ordination) because the powers and responsibilities of the ordained were separated from a congregation in a local church. Unique authority to administer the means of grace, the sacraments, which determined the communicant's future life or death, gave the clergy immense power in a society where the belief was almost universal that the gateway to heaven or hell was controlled by the church.

The greatness of the medieval Catholic idea of ordination was its conviction of the objectivity of the priestly ministry.

According to this view, God's grace was given in the act of ordination through the laying on of hands and the invocation of the Holy Spirit in such a way that there was objective alteration of the ordinand. The priest was empowered to convey God's grace through the objective reality of the sacraments. The sacraments themselves were understood to be operative, through the words and actions of the priest, apart from human experience or inclination, and even apart from a congregation of believers. This was how the "private Mass" was justified, where priests celebrated Mass alone, supported by financial payments from lay people who bought such services to curry favor with God. Thus the greatness of the idea of ordination also opened the door to some of the worst aspects of medieval Christianity.

The power of ordained ministers to exercise decisive determination about a believer's salvation allowed practices to arise which enhanced clerical status, institutional church wealth and ecclesiastical power. Clergy dominated the church as the church dominated the society. Priests often were ignorant of the Bible and participant in a system of church order which victimized lay people by depriving them of the scriptures and selling the favors of the church's ministry, including forgiveness of sins, in crude transactions which made the church rich in worldly things. Bishops took on the trappings of princes and indulged themselves with palaces, fine clothes and rich adornments of office.

The Protestant Reformation of the sixteenth century included a frontal attack on the understanding of ministry which had permitted clerical authority and privilege to become oppressive. The Reformation is characterized by three chief centers of activity: Germany, Switzerland and England. These also correspond with major intellectual traditions; the Reformation in Germany is identified particularly with Martin Luther, while the Swiss Reformation is especially identified with John Calvin. The English Reformation is different because it is not linked with a great theological thinker, and because it developed as an act of state, rather than as a complex theological movement. Each of the main Reformation traditions dealt with ministry and ordination.

Methodism emerged two centuries later, in the eighteenth century, within Anglicanism, so we have particular interest in the Anglican Reformation. Because of John Wesley's own family background and experience, however, Methodism also was influenced by European Pietism and Puritanism and, therefore, it is important for us to note the main ideas of the Continental Reformation in regard to ministry.

The Continental Reformers were convinced that a return to the New Testament required a fundamentally altered understanding of the church's ministry. Their attack on medieval Catholic teachings and practices of ministry emphasized the ministry of the whole people of God. The phrase "priesthood of all believers" refers to the corporate ministry of the body of Christ in the world. It does not, however, eliminate functional distinctions among Christians, or obliterate the necessity for the church to set some apart for the particular service of ordained ministry.

Protestants insisted upon the rejection of ordination as a sacrament. They also rejected the view that ordination results in a permanent, indelible character change, priestly power to forgive sin, the idea that the powers conferred in ordination are unrelated to specific congregations of Christian faithful, and sacramental celebration apart from congregations of believers. The Continental Reformers set forth positive affirmations about ordained ministry which they believed to be based on the authority of the canonical scriptures of the Old and New Testaments.[29]

The role of the ordained minister involved preaching and the administration of the sacraments. The Reformers reacted against the almost exclusive emphasis on sacramental ministries in medieval Catholicism. Their rediscovery of the Bible was coupled with a passionate concern for the preached word. Luther wrote:

Three great abuses have befallen the service of God. First, God's Word is not proclaimed; there is only reading and singing in the churches. Second, because God's Word has been suppressed, many unchristian inventions and lies have sneaked into the service of reading, singing and preaching, and they are horrible to see. Third, such service to God is being undertaken as a good work by which one hopes to obtain God's grace and salvation. Thus faith has perished and everyone wishes to endow churches or to become a priest, monk or nun.[30]

Only faithful preaching of God's Word in the congregation could help to prevent the church from falling into error.

The ordained minister was given authority to preach the word and interpret the Bible in the congregation. Although the Reformers rejected the priestly ministry, they did not abandon the idea of ordination. In principle all Christian believers could read and interpret the scriptures, but some were set apart to function as teachers, preachers and ministers of the sacraments on behalf of the body of Christ.

The congregation was to choose its preacher and the authority of ordained ministerial leadership derived from, and was related to, the congregation being served. Both Luther and Calvin had a role for other presbyters in examining, approving and ordaining ministers, but the essential point is that the Continental Reformers provided a clear alternative to the idea of ordination to a "status" which was not directly related to ministry in a congregation. They thus rejected the "absolute ordination" of the Roman Catholic Church.

The Reformers did away with the hierarchical three-fold ministry of deacons, presbyters and bishops and advocated one ordination, to the presbyterate, which was administered by other presbyters. This they believed to be more scriptural than the elaborate pattern characteristic of medieval Catholicism. The argument for one presbyteral ordination was the result of strong antipathy toward the episcopacy and the excesses of pomp and pride which accompanied the office in medieval Europe. A reformed and purified church was to model itself as much as possible after the New Testament. No pope, cardinals, archbishops or bishops were found there, so reform of the ministry required simplification and the elimination of hierarchy.

The Protestant ministry entailed education to a degree not required in the Catholic priesthood. While it was the case that education was the province of the church in medieval Europe, it was also true that the average priest was often ignorant. As long as he could say the Latin Mass, he could function. The Continental Reformers maintained the need for education because of their insistence on the central role of the Bible. To interpret the Bible through preaching and teaching, it was necessary for the ordained minister to know the scriptures and to study commentaries and other scholarly works. The image of the preacher, especially for Calvin, was the scholar-teacher. The preacher was to teach the people so that they, too, could read the Bible and understand the faith.

Ordination in early Protestantism was a functional office in the church related to a specific congregation of believers. There was no notion of a change of "status" which gave the ordained minister power to communicate the grace of God through the sacraments without regard to matters of character, ability, or gifts for the office. The issue of suitable moral stature was therefore central. The church cared about moral character because its leaders needed to reflect the gospel they proclaimed in the wholeness of their living. The authenticity of the ministry was in part related to its manifestation in the lives of the clergy. Calvin says it succinctly: "To sum up, only those are to be chosen who are of sound doctrine and of holy life, not notorious in any fault which might both deprive them of authority and disgrace the ministry."[31] The Continental Reformers were responsible for a new conception of Christian ministry which sought at once to be biblically sound, attentive to church tradition and appropriate for the times.

The Reformation in England is not identified with the reforming zeal of any major theological thinker, but instead was a combination of political, economic, intellectual and religious factors resulting in the official break with the Roman Catholic Church and the inauguration of the Church of England. The Reformation Parliament (1529-1536), through a series of official acts, established a church which was free of foreign control, but which left largely unaltered the idea and practice of ministry. In this book we cannot go into an extensive analysis of the English Reformation, but we need to examine the implications of it for ministry by noticing several major principles.[32]

The first is nationality. The Church of England was defined by its identity with the English state, monarchy, language, and customs. A major objection to the Roman Catholic Church was that one of England's major institutions, an institution which had vast land holdings, significant political influence and which shaped and determined life and death, was under the ultimate control of men who were not English. At a time when the Roman Catholic Church was a formidable political, economic and military force, and when sentiments of nationalism were growing, it was not difficult for the King and Parliament to secure support for the official severance of the English church from Rome.

A second principle was that of continuity. It was the position of the English Reformers that a break with Rome would not affect fundamental continuity with the apostolic tradition. They did not question the idea of episcopal succession, and argued that the rejection of the papacy did not cause rupture in the succession. The Reformation in England was an effort to make the Catholic Church English; only as time went on did it become clear that such an idea was not easy to implement. Continuity also applied to worship style and practice. Archbishop Thomas Cranmer's *Book of Common Prayer*, of 1549, was a new service book for the English church and a compromise between medieval Catholicism and Protestantism. Although there was a break with Rome, there was also a fundamental continuity in ministry and worship which has always been a hallmark of the Church of England.

The third principle was that of uniformity. The prevailing idea was that unity in the state required uniformity in the church. Accordingly, the *Book of Common Prayer* became the standard of practice for the church's ministry. The fact that there was diversity of opinion about theological matters in the church made it all the more obvious that uniformity in language, liturgy and theology was necessary. The idea that uniformity was necessary was related to the principles of nationality and state supremacy.

State supremacy was the fourth principle of the English Reformation. When papal control over the Christian church in England was ended, the pope was replaced by the monarch. The Act of Supremacy (1534) made Henry VIII the "Protector and Only Supreme Head of the Church and Clergy of England." The contrast between the Continental Reformation and the Reformation in England is particularly sharp here. In England, there was no challenge to the notion of hierarchy in the church and, therefore, the Catholic understanding of ministry was left in place, only the king was at the top instead of the pope. The reality of state supremacy meant that the church would be subject to upheaval anytime political changes took place, and perpetual struggle over theology and practice would trouble the church as England experienced turmoil in government.

The seventeenth century was particularly turbulent as ideas inspired by the Continental Reformation brought about revolution which ended the monarchy and altered the ministry of the church by eliminating bishops between the years 1649 and 1660. It is significant for this study that the principles of nationality, continuity, uniformity and state supremacy were not challenged. Thus, although specific manifestations of the church changed, the basic assumptions did not. By the end of the century, just prior to the birth of John Wesley, a Protestant monarchy was in place, and the Church of England once again had an episcopal polity, and basically Catholic form of ministry, in which bishops governed the church and presided at the ordinations of presbyters and deacons.

This overview of the complex history of ministry in Christianity has taken us from the early church to the beginning of the eighteenth century. The point of the survey has been to notice on the one hand that ministry is very diverse because it is shaped by the particularities of circumstance, as well as by theological thought and ecclesiastical practice, and on the other hand, that despite the diversity, there are evident continuities.

Wholeness in Ministry

An overview of the history of Christian ministry exhibits a number of points of continuity which contribute to our understanding of the ministry of the whole people of God.

1. The entire history of the church demonstrates a concern for specific and organized leadership for worship and for teaching, including the teaching of doctrine and practice.

2. There is no one scriptural model for leadership, but certain scriptural themes and concepts have consistently shaped church thinking about ministerial leadership.

3. The three-fold pattern of deacons, presbyters (or elders), and bishops early became the dominant structure for ministry in the church, though the exact relationship among the three developed slowly and differed in various centers of the early church. The linking of sacramental ministries to presbyters and bishops had to do with the need for unity in Christian teaching and came about very early. Ordination authorized one "officially" to represent the church. Later, Roman Catholic sacramental theology would propose that ordination resulted in an indelible character change in the ordinand and that one was ordained to a "status" which was unrelated to any specific place or work. This view, linked with an exaggeration of the distinction between laity and clergy, and an emphasis on the power of the clergy over sin and death, contributed to a corrupt clericalism in medieval Catholicism.

4. The Protestant Reformation made reform of the ministry one of its chief concerns. The Continental Reformers insisted that scripture did not allow the kind of three-fold ministry pattern dominant in Roman Catholicism. They argued that the *episkopos* and the *presbyteros* were functionally the same and that ministry made sense only in specific relationship to a congregation. Ordination was therefore viewed as authorization to teach and administer the sacraments. The dominant tradi-

43

tions of the Protestant Reformation did not challenge the need for ministerial leadership or its relationship to the sacraments, even as they emphasized preaching and understood ordination as authorization from the church to minister in the congregation.

5. The Church of England, the product of the English Reformation, maintained the Catholic three-fold pattern of ministry with deacons, presbyters and bishops. A strong Protestant movement in the seventeenth century sought radical reform, including the elimination of episcopacy, but ultimately the traditional pattern prevailed, despite continuing debate as to whether there was a theological difference between presbyters and bishops. The Anglican conception of ordained ministry was influenced by both the Catholic and Reformed traditions.

6. Most Christians belong to churches in which a specific three-fold pattern of ministry prevails. The theological understanding of orders of ministry are diverse, but the dominant model involves ministry of deacons, presbyters and bishops. Virtually all Christians belong to churches in which there is provision for "set apart" leadership and in which the functions of deacons, presbyters and bishops are provided for, even though the nomenclature may be different. Obviously the theological differences are significant, but the point is that the scriptural provisions for leadership, service, and oversight in the community of Jesus Christ is manifested in all churches.

7. All Christians are called to the ministry of the church, but not all ministries are the same.

There are varieties of ministries within the church, all of which derive from Jesus Christ, in whom the several ministries are fundamentally unified. Ordained ministries do not represent a "downfall" from a "pristine" state of charismatic ministries. The idea that the church ought to recover its early innocence represented by the kind of ministries I cited from Paul is a theological mistake. The gift of God's Holy Spirit allowed the church to organize itself, so that it could function and serve in the world. This is the meaning of incarnation. As God became human in Christ to live in the world, so the church, as the body of Christ, becomes a human organization in the world. It is not only a human organization, it is also divine, "Dearly beloved the Church is of God."[33] The church is divine and human; as such its ministries find their initiation in Christ and are a gift of God through the grace of the Holy Spirit to the world.

The priesthood of all believers means that the church continues the priesthood of Christ who "did not exalt himself" (Heb. 5:5). The nature of this priesthood is a self-emptying service characteristic of all authentic Christian ministry, both general and ordained. The general ministry and the ordained ministry should never be thought of as being in conflict because they share the same servant character. There is complementarity and interdependence between the general and ordained ministries.

The complementarity of all Christian ministries is an important theological concept. To assert that all Christians are ministers is not to "put down" the clergy. It is to remind us of the complex interaction between laity and clergy. To assert the importance and integrity of the clergy is not to "put down" the laity; rather it is to recognize distinctions of functions in the community. This chapter has described the reasons for the distinction between laity and clergy and has shown the development of ministry in the history of the church. I have told this history in the context of the theological concept of wholeness to remind us that lay persons have honorable and vital ministries and that ordination is seriously misunderstood if it is thought that clergy are more important or central to the church. Similarly, it is wrong not to appreciate the legitimate contributions of the ordained. Perhaps the most important thing to be learned from this chapter is that, at its best, the church has dealt with ministry not in terms of power, rights or privileges, but in terms of service and giving.[34] Through the grace of the Lord Jesus Christ, and the gift of the Holy Spirit, ministry is given to the church for the sake of the world. Though we are not all the same, we are all one, and we are all dependent upon God and called to make our wills conform to God's will. Our equality in ministry is in our subjectivity to God. We do not share "rights," we share common subjection to God. We all are equally needful; and, like Christ, we do not exalt ourselves, but we seek humble obedience to God's will. This is the key to the ministry of the whole people of God.

Chapter III
The Development of Ministry in the Wesleyan Tradition

... our sufficiency is from God, who has qualified us to be ministers of a new covenant, not in a written code, but in the Spirit; for the written code kills, but the Spirit gives life.

–2 Corinthians 3:5-6

To understand the place of the Wesleyan conception of ministry in the larger picture of the history of Christian ministry, one must begin with eighteenth century Anglicanism. The English Reformation, unlike that of the Continent, produced a state church which retained the Catholic three orders of ministry, deacons, presbyters, and bishops. Deacons read the scriptures and preached, but the diaconate was basically a first order in which one prepared for presbyteral ordination. Rights and responsibilities for both preaching and sacramental ministries belonged to presbyters and bishops. Ordination to both offices required the laying on of hands by a bishop, who, it was believed, was in direct succession to the apostolic witnesses of the original ministries of Jesus Christ and teachings of the Church.

Although Protestant Puritan voices within the seventeenth century Church of England challenged episcopal government as unscriptural and caused major turmoil, episcopal authority prevailed. In the eighteenth century, episcopal polity was not a significant issue of contention for Anglicans, and since church

Church government was coupled to the state, the rules governing the orders and practice of ministry were thought essential for civil welfare. The Church was a dominant institution because it was established as an arm of the state, but, on the whole, it lacked vitality, perhaps in part because its clergy were participants in a staid system which did not encourage or demand creative leadership. While John Wesley frontally attacked the lack of Christian vitality in the Church, and the quality of its clergy, he assumed the Anglican context. He never left the Church and he defended its theological structure as both apostolic and scriptural.[1] At the same time he introduced innovations he judged essential to mission, which were contrary to Anglican practice. Wesley's theology of ministry evidences a commitment to both the Catholic tradition as expressed in Anglicanism and to the evangelical insistence that gospel ministry is not restricted to any ecclesiastical structure.

John Wesley's Understanding of Ministry

John Wesley's father, Samuel, was an Anglican clergyman and his mother, Susanna, a devout lay woman. Both came to Anglicanism by choice and were convinced of the correctness of Anglican polity and practice despite deep family roots in dissenting Puritanism. Susanna's father, Dr. Samuel Annesley, was a prominent Puritan minister who was ejected from his London pulpit in 1662 because of his non-conformist views. Susanna's religious views did not conform to her father's, and she became an Anglican when she was thirteen years old. Samuel was ordained in 1690 and spent forty five years as a priest of the Church of England. John Wesley's early understanding of ministry was rooted and shaped in an Anglican context.

After graduation from Christ Church College, Oxford University, in 1724, Wesley prepared for Holy Orders and was ordained a deacon on Sunday, September 19, 1725, by Bishop John Potter in Christ Church Cathedral, Oxford. Bishop Potter ordained him a priest on September 22, 1728, also in Oxford.

Throughout his life Wesley was a priest of the Church of England, though he never served a conventional parish as the priest-in-charge. His earliest regular service was as a Fellow of Lincoln College, Oxford. In this role he taught logic, Greek, philosophy and disputation. It was also during this period that Wesley was involved with a group of devout young men who were called "Methodists" because of their enthusiasm for exacting practices intended to perfect them in Christian living. John's younger brother Charles was instrumental in forming this "Holy Club," but John became its leader. The members engaged in fasting, frequent Holy Communion, and various social service ministries, including jail ministry. This Oxford period, the so-called "first rise of Methodism," is important because it evidences a number of the major characteristics of later Methodism, including small group emphasis, seriousness in Bible study and worship, regular reception of Holy Communion, careful attention to personal habits of holy living, and social service as a necessary part of Christian faith.[2]

The rigor of his outward practices did not nourish his spiritual needs, and Wesley was frustrated and unhappy in his Christianity. Largely as a result of his anxieties about his own religious life, Wesley agreed to an unlikely assignment for a well-educated and serious Oxford Fellow when he accepted the invitation of Dr. John Burton, trustee of the Georgia colony and patron of the Society for the Propagation of the Gospel, and General James Oglethorpe, Governor of Georgia, to serve as a missionary priest in Savannah. He sailed on October 21, 1735, along with his brother Charles and two other Oxford Methodists, Benjamin Ingham and Charles Delamotte. Wesley set out to do Christian service, but his motive was selfish. He hoped that the experience would confirm and strengthen him in Christian faith. In a letter to Dr. John Burton he wrote that he went to save his soul:

> My chief motive to which all the rest are subordinate, is the hope of saving my own soul. I hope to learn the true sense of the gospel of Christ by preaching it to the heathens. They have no comments to construe away the text . . . . From these, therefore,

I hope to learn the purity of that faith which was once delivered
to the saints . . . .[3]

During his one year and nine months in Georgia, Wesley
accomplished little in ministry to the Native Americans and
most of his work was with the English colonists. The experience
was a failure. He sought to impose on them the exacting practices of the Oxford Methodists. This "second rise of
Methodism" continued Wesley's interest in worship experi-
mentation, including the preparation and publication of a *Collection of Psalms and Hymns*.[4] His strict rules for Christian living
did not sit well with the hardened colonists in the rough
Georgia colony. His ministry lacked pastoral sensitivity and he
even allowed his official responsibilities to be clouded by personal issues as he worked through a disastrous relationship
with a young woman named Sophy Hopkey. A broken and
unhappy man, Wesley left America on December 22, 1737.
During the winter crossing to England, he wrote in his Journal
on January 24, 1738:

> I went to America to convert the Indians; but, oh, who shall
> convert me? Who, what is he that will deliver me from this evil
> heart of unbelief?[5]

The Georgia experience did not do for Wesley what he
hoped. It made his anxieties more severe as he realized that his
ministry suffered from a lack of authenticity. He was a serious
and responsible ordained minister of the gospel of Jesus Christ,
but his ministry was unsatisfying to himself and ineffective
with others.

Back in England, Wesley continued his fretful quest for religious assurance through reading, prayer, and the founding,
along with Moravian Peter Boehler, of the "Fetter Lane Society," a small group of serious, devout persons. Wesley would
later refer to this as the "third rise of Methodism." Resolution
of his own religious anxieties came in May of 1738 when he experienced the personal conviction of God's grace in Jesus

Christ. Writing about his experience of May 24, 1738, Wesley says:

> In the evening I went very unwillingly to a society in Aldersgate Street, where one was reading Luther's Preface to the Epistle to the Romans. About a quarter before nine, while he was describing the change which God works in the heart through faith in Christ, I felt my heart strangely warmed. I felt I did trust in Christ, Christ alone for salvation; and an assurance was given me that He had taken away my sins, even mine, and saved me from the law of sin and death.[6]

Wesley's "Aldersgate experience" has received a great deal of attention, and it was a central event in his life. There had been much preparation for it during prior years of ministry, and there would be moments of faithful doubt and despair following it. Aldersgate came to function as a symbol in Wesley's ministry, and it has served as a symbol ever since for Methodists. Aldersgate represents the coming of authenticity to Wesley's ministry. After Aldersgate, Wesley was freed from obsessive concern for himself, and therefore able to proclaim the gospel of Jesus Christ with assurance. Aldersgate worked a change in Wesley that was more than personal. The change had implications for his ministry and for his understanding of Christian ministry.

John Wesley became a central figure in the eighteenth century evangelical revival in England because his Aldersgate experience, and subsequent spiritual growth, convinced him that God gave him an "extra-ordinary" ministry.[7] The ordinary ministry of the church was through its established parish system, but Wesley was not a parish priest, and his ministry of revival was carried on as an itinerant. When the pulpits of parish churches were closed to him, he preached out-of-doors. When educated and sophisticated people found him embarrassing, he turned to the poor and dispossessed. He went to the cities and industrial towns where the people were and did not confine his work to normal ecclesiastical patterns. His famous affirmation about the world being his parish is not about world missions but about his itinerant ministry.

> Man forbids me to do this in another's parish: that is, in effect to do it at all; seeing I have now no parish of my own, nor probably ever shall. Whom, then, shall I hear, God or man? . . . Suffer me now to tell you my principles in this matter. I look upon all the world as my parish; thus far I mean, that in whatever part of it I am I judge it meet, right, and my bounden duty to declare, unto all that are willing to hear, the glad tidings of salvation. This is the work which I know God has called me to; and sure I am that His blessings attend it.[8]

Wesley's conviction that he was not to be an "ordinary" priest of the church, but instead an "extra-ordinary" messenger of the gospel informed all aspects of his ministry and theology.

Methodism was a reform movement within the Anglican Church, and the primary criterion for judging every aspect of its ministry was evangelical witness. It is often said of Methodism that pragmatic concerns of ministry take priority over fine points of theology. In a sense this is true, but it is important to understand that there is a theological reason for the priority, namely evangelical mission. The conviction of his "extra-ordinary" ministry to proclaim the saving power of Jesus Christ would inform all of Wesley's judgments in regard to ministry. Although he never systematically articulated a doctrine of ministry, six points can be made about his theology of ministry.

1. *Wesley recognized a preaching ministry apart from ordained ministry.* While Wesley criticized the vitality and quality of the ordained ministry, he never challenged ordination itself. One of his major innovations, however, was the insistence that preaching was not confined to ordained ministry. The chief distinguishing feature of ordination was its relationship to sacramental ministries.

It must never be thought that Wesley downplayed the sacraments, and especially the Eucharist. Methodism stood for a sacramental revival within the church, and some of Charles

Wesley's most magnificent hymns were written for Eucharistic services. The Wesleys never waivered, of course, from church teaching that only ordained ministers administer the sacraments. They made a distinction between sacramental ministries and preaching.

John Wesley's recognition of the validity of lay preaching was the result of his conviction that lay persons effectively brought men and women to the saving knowledge of Jesus Christ. Wesley never tired of pointing to successful examples of lay preaching in the evangelical revival. In his staunch defense of the practice he appealed to the early church and Reformation as well:

> . . . were not most of those whom it pleased God to employ in promoting the Reformation abroad, laymen also? Could that great work have been promoted at all in many places, if laymen had not preached?[9]

The lay preachers of Methodism were a remarkable force of disciplined men who were approved by Wesley and appointed by him to ministry within the connection.

2. *Wesley insisted that all authentic ministry requires an inward call from God.* He distinguished between the call to ministry from God, the "inward call," and the call to ministry from the church, the "outward call." Among Anglicans of his day emphasis in ministry tended to be upon formal education and ordination to Holy Orders. In ordination the Holy Spirit empowered the ordinand to exercise the ministry of Word and Sacrament and the outward acts of ministry were not necessarily related to the inward spiritual life of the ordained minister. Wesley himself functioned as a priest of the church for ten years prior to Aldersgate. His own experience convinced him that authentic ministry requires the inward conviction of rebirth in Jesus Christ and call from God.

The main point of Wesley's insistence on the inward call has to do with the evangelical conviction that authenticity in ministry requires that the minister has accepted the free gift of

God's salvation in Jesus Christ for himself or herself and feels the inward call from God to preach. Preferably the outward call from the church will accompany the inward call from God, but, to make his point of the priority of the evangelical experience, Wesley stresses the inward call:

> I allow that it is highly expedient whoever preaches in his name should have an outward as well as an inward call; but that it is absolutely necessary I deny.[10]

3. *Wesley believed that the moral lives of pastors should be exemplary.* From the time of Methodism's beginning in Oxford stress was placed on holy living. Wesley united the theological emphases of justification and sanctification and expected Methodists to be "going on to perfection." Pastors of the flock of Jesus Christ are to be examples of holy living to the church and to the world:

> They are supposed to go before the flock (as in the manner of the eastern shepherds to this day) and to guide them in all the ways of truth and holiness . . . .[11]

The exemplary nature of lay and ordained ministers was taken for granted in early Methodism and discipline was strictly enforced. The questions in *The Discipline*, which have been asked of all Methodist preachers from the earliest days of the movement, evidence strong concern for rigor in the moral life.

4. *Wesley believed that the authenticity of ministry was to be judged by its fruits.* The fruits of Christian ministry included souls saved, new members received, new classes begun and engagement in social service ministries (such as care for the sick and dying, jail work and education). Wesley was a great keeper of records and recorder of the progress of Methodism. His ministry prior to Aldersgate was characterized by rigidity and dogmatism. He was devout, disciplined and determined, but he lacked a sensitive appreciation for the flexibility that can bring positive results in ministry. The evangelical priority

meant that the test of authenticity would be effectiveness. This was what allowed him to engage in open-air preaching, extemporary prayer and to make use of lay preachers. It was also the impetus for allowing women to preach. He determined that their effectiveness in ministry must be a gift from God. Early Methodism had a significant group of women in leadership roles because Wesley tested ministry by its fruits.[12]

5. *Wesley believed in a connectional ministry which is appointed and disciplined.* As a renewal movement within the Anglican Church, the preachers of early Methodism were somewhat analogous to the monastic orders committed to the renewal of the Church within Roman Catholicism. They functioned as a disciplined cadre of persons whose lives were wholly committed to the revitalization of the Church through evangelical revival. Wesley developed a connectional system of rigorous expectations, strict accountability, and clear authority.[13]

Methodism was built on the theological conviction that preaching the gospel was the single priority. Preaching converted sinners and guided members of the flock of Jesus Christ in their efforts to perfect their lives through the grace of the Holy Spirit, in the process of sanctification. All else was subjected to this end, including, and especially, the personal needs and wants of the ministry. Only a system that placed the preachers according to the strategic needs of the entire connection could be acceptable, and no system that allowed for dissention and controversy among leadership or people would be tolerated. The answer was the power of appointment to which preachers and members agreed.

It is crucial to understand that the ideas of appointment and discipline were not in the first place matters of structure, polity, organization or strategy for Wesley and the early Methodists. At base these derived from theological convictions concerning discipline, connection and appointment. A major contention of Wesleyan theology is that all Christian men and women are placed in their work by God. Wesley's Covenant Service, which dates from 1755, and which may be his greatest piece of liturgical writing, is the clearest and most moving expression of the

Methodist theological position about "place." In the service the minister makes a statement about the nature of Christian service, as it applies to all believers:

> And now, beloved, let us bind ourselves with willing bonds to our covenant God, and take the yoke of Christ upon us.
>
> This taking of his yoke upon us means that we are heartily content that he appoint us our place and work, and he alone be our reward.
>
> Christ has many services to be done; some are easy, others are difficult; some bring honor, others bring reproach; some are suitable to our natural inclinations, and temporal interests, others are contrary to both. In some we may please Christ and please ourselves; in others we cannot please Christ except by denying ourselves. Yet the power to do all these things is assuredly given us in Christ, who strengthens us.[14]

This clear expression of the Wesleyan understanding of Christian ministry has several key elements.

All Christian believers are called to ministry and appointed to ministries by God. Entry into Christ's service is by choice. God has given men and women free will, and by God's grace we are free to "take the yoke of Christ upon us." Therefore the bonds which bind us to God, and to Christ's service, are "willing bonds." Once we have bound ourselves to God in Jesus Christ, then we content ourselves that God "appoint us our place and work."

This theological view of the nature of the Christian's appointment to service is expressed in Charles Wesley's great hymn for the Covenant Service:

> Move, and actuate, and guide,
> Divers gifts to each divide;
> Placed according to thy will,
> Let us all our work fulfill.[15]

Wesley here picks up the Pauline view of ministry expressed in 1 Corinthians 12:11 which we examined in the last chapter.

Early Methodists, under the leadership of the Wesley's, perceived the active work of God in their lives to the extent that they viewed their station in life and their work to be part of God's plan for the total ministry. This understanding must be seen in relation to another great Wesleyan teaching about human participation in salvation through sanctifying grace. Thus while our station in life is a mystery of God's grace, it is not the case that there is nothing we can do about it. We accept our station and seek to grow in grace to fulfill the work God gives us. We must also remember that Methodists had a great sense of community and individual accountability to the community. Accordingly faithfulness in carrying out appointed tasks is judged by the community. In the case of early Methodism this was through the classes and bands for the laity and through the conference, headed by Wesley, for the preachers.

In the case of the preachers, the Wesleyan theology of service translated into the idea of appointment. Appointment was intended to strengthen the work of the movement because it allowed mission to be the determining factor in the stationing of the preachers rather than personal desire or the preferences of the people. Wesley's itinerants freely conformed their wills to the will of the movement embodied in Wesley himself. A hallmark of Methodist ministry, as articulated by Wesley, is the trust that God's will is worked out in the appointment process, even if that is sometimes hard to see. The theological significance of appointment is that one submits to the corporate will of the church, represented by the one to whom power of appointment is given, and such submission is characteristic of the church in relation to Jesus Christ.

Appointment is related to Wesley's conviction about the connectional character of all authentic Christian ministry. The body of Jesus Christ is not a local reality but a corporate connection transcending any particular local manifestation. Here Wesley took Paul's image of the church as the body of Christ (1 Cor. 12:12) literally. Methodism exemplified the inter-related character of Christian believers and communities. Just as every Christian community is a part of the larger connection, so every

Christian minister is tied to the larger ministry. There is no such thing as an "independent" Christian community or minister. Christianity is not a do-it-yourself operation. This principle was the cornerstone of Wesley's thinking about the nature of the church. His articulation and implementation of this principle is one of his enduring contributions to ecumenical Christianity.[16]

There have always been objections to the notion of the theology of appointment, and some of the problems it occasions in practice. Later in this book we will examine the idea as it is translated into American episcopal Methodism. That human frailty and sin is present in the actual working out of the theology of appointment goes with the recognition that the church is both human and divine. Nevertheless, any effort to understand the Wesleyan theology of ministry must acknowledge the central role played by the concepts of discipline, appointment, and connection.

6. *Wesley affirmed the ministerial orders of the Church of England, but denied that they are absolute.* As we have seen, John Wesley's understanding of ministry was rooted in Anglicanism. His relationship to the Church of England is complex because he always remained within it, but led a movement which became increasingly alienated from it during his life and finally separated from it after his death. The full story of Wesley's relationship to his own church is too complicated to deal with in this book.[17] His views about Anglican orders must be understood, however, if one is to comprehend ordination in Methodism.

Wesley did not question the three orders of ministry, although he did claim, on the basis of Christian history, that presbyters and bishops are theologically of the same order, and that the chief distinguishing feature of the episcopacy is its function of oversight (superintendence). This idea was not new to Wesley. As I demonstrated in the last chapter, the debate about the relationship between the presbyterate and episcopate is an old one in Christianity and was recurrent within Anglicanism.

Wesley's view therefore was not unique, though the fact that he ultimately acted on it when he ordained men for America, made him unique.

Toward the end of his life the pressures on Wesley in regard to separation from the Church of England were very great. There were always Anglican clergy who were part of the Methodist movement, but most clergy of the Church of England did not appreciate Methodists and did not make much effort to provide pastoral care. In turn the Methodists did not seek relationship with the parish churches and preferred to receive pastoral care from their own unordained preachers. Despite its lack of ordained ministers, Methodism increasingly was functioning as a separate body even as Wesley maintained the official, and for him absolute, position that Methodists were not "dissenters" and that the movement functioned within the church.[18]

While he remained loyal to the Church, and affirmed the authority of its doctrines and worship, Wesley was not willing to ascribe the same authority to its polity. This was because he insisted that scripture is the primary authority, and he distinguished between that which is prescribed in scripture, and that which is scriptural: "As to my own judgment, I still believe 'the Episcopal form of Church government to be both scriptural and apostolical': I mean, well agreeing with the practice and writings of the Apostles. But that it is prescribed in Scripture I do not believe."[19] This distinction allowed for the view that Anglican orders of ministry were fully consistent with apostolic faith, but that apostolic faith did not depend on any precise form of ecclesiastical organization.

Wesley's Ordinations for America

John Wesley's understanding of ministerial orders emerged from a complex interaction of his personal rootage in the Church of England, his study of the history of Christianity, his evangelical theological convictions, and his religious and ecclesiastical experience. Because he kept such a detailed account of his own life in his *Journal*, we know that his reading influenced his views about ministerial orders and ordination. He credits two books as having particular influence. In 1746, he read Lord Peter King's book, *Account of the Primitive Church*. King tells the story of the development of ministerial orders and makes the point that the early church had no one pattern of polity or ministry. Furthermore, King argues that the church in Alexandria was a specific example of presbyters electing and ordaining bishops after the death of a former bishop. The point of King's argument is that presbyters and bishops are of the same order, and that they differ by function. Functionally presbyters are inferior because bishops are given superintending responsibility. Wesley espouses King's judgment: "I read over Lord King's *Account of the Primitive Church*. In spite of the vehement prejudice of my education, I was ready to believe that this was a fair and impartial draught; but, if so, it would follow that bishops and presbyters are (essentially) of one order . . . ."[20]

The second book Wesley cites is *Irenicum* by Bishop Samuel Stillingfleet. Stillingfleet also argues that there is no scripturally sanctioned pattern of church government and that originally there was no essential theological difference between the role of presbyters and bishops. The development of ministerial orders was gradual and the emergence of the episcopacy as the superior order was natural and useful, but not fundamental to Christian faith. In a letter written in 1756, Wesley refers to Stillingfleet: "I think he has unanswerably proved that neither Christ or His apostles prescribed any particular form of church government, and that the plea for the divine right of Episcopacy was never heard of in the primitive Church."[21]

As we saw in the last chapter, modern scholarship dealing with the history and theology of ministry demonstrates the accuracy of Wesley's judgments. The New Testament does not prescribe one form of church polity, and the three-fold order of ordained ministries developed gradually in the church. That the presbyterate and episcopate were not always in a hierarchical relationship to one another is generally accepted. How particular church traditions interpret this historical information is another matter. Ordination in Methodism derives from Wesley's judgments and actions. He always held the view that only ordained ministers could administer the sacraments, but the practical reality of the relationship between the Church of England and the Methodist movement presented a serious problem. The needs of Methodists were not being met by ordained ministers. Despite Wesley's intellectual convictions about Anglican orders of ministry, he did not challenge them within the English context until very late in his life, and then only under extreme pressure from his movement. He consistently denied that his actions ever separated him or Methodism from the Church of England. It was the need for ordained ministers for sacramental ministry that brought Wesley to his controversial decision to ordain men for America.

The beginnings of Methodism in the American colonies came in the 1760's through the arrival of English Methodist lay men and women. Soon they were joined by lay preachers sent by Wesley. Francis Asbury, later to be the real founder of American episcopal Methodism, came to North America as a lay preacher in 1771, when he was twenty-four years old. During this early period, the lay preachers looked to Wesley for leadership, although even before 1784 Asbury began gradually to assume priority as Wesley's "assistant," in American Methodism. The Revolutionary War was a difficult period because popular perception viewed Methodism with suspicion since it was an English movement and its head, Wesley, was a fiercely loyal Englishman utterly opposed to the Revolution. While most Anglican clergy and Methodist itinerants went home prior to the war, Asbury remained and was able to revive the movement. The chief problem he faced was the lack of ordained ministers. Methodists wanted the sacraments and they had no where to turn. There were few Anglican clergymen and no bishop in the new nation. Members of the English state church were more alienated in the free air of America than were the Methodists. Asbury and the American Methodists urgently requested that provision be made for ordained ministers. In 1784, there were 14,998 Methodists in the United States being served by eighty-three non-ordained, itinerant Methodist preachers.[22]

The situation created a leadership crisis. Wesley insisted that only ordained persons could administer the sacraments, and the American Methodists agreed. There were some who argued for a break with Wesley, not on the question of the necessity of ordination, but on the question of authority to ordain. A movement to institute presbyteral ordination for America was attempted at the Fluvanna Conference in Virginia. Against the will of Wesley and Asbury, a small group of Methodist preachers formed a "presbytery" and ordained each other. Ultimately those loyal to Wesley prevailed, but it was clear that action had to be taken or Asbury and Wesley would lose control altogether. Wesley faced a new and difficult situation in America where Methodists were on equal footing with other religious groups (there was no established national church) and where reference to Anglicanism for sacramental ministries was impossible. Wesley asked the Bishop of London to ordain some of his preachers for America, but the Bishop refused.

At this point Wesley relied on his historical and theological knowledge, and his practical sense, to solve the problem. His theological convictions led him to take the extraordinary step of creating a new church for the American continent and ordaining and appointing men to lead it. The facts are as follows: At 4:00 a.m. on September 1, 1784, in Bristol, Wesley ordained Richard Whatcoat and Thomas Vasey deacons and on September 2 ordained them elders and appointed them to serve in America.[23] He also "ordained" Thomas Coke, who was already an elder (presbyter) of the Church of England, a "superintendent" and appointed him and Francis Asbury to serve as superintendents of the new church in the United States. Wesley directed that Coke was to ordain Asbury, and that they were to ordain others for service among the American Methodists. In the Diary for September 2, 1794, Wesley wrote: "Prayed, ordained Dr. Coke as a Superintendent, by the imposition of hands and prayer (being assisted by other ordained ministers)."[24]

The actions Wesley took in regard to ordination were unprecedented because within the canons of the Church of England a presbyter had no right to ordain. Remember, however, that as early as 1746, when he read King's book, *Account of the Primitive Church*, Wesley had concluded that presbyters and bishops were essentially of the same order, and that the priority of bishops was functional. We have seen that from the time of Aldersgate on, Wesley regarded himself as serving an extraordinary ministry, and, as leader of the Methodists, he was functioning as a bishop in the scriptural sense. Certainly he was an elder in the church functioning as a "superintendent" or exercising "oversight" over a portion of the church. In a letter to his brother Charles in June, 1780, he wrote: "I verily believe I have as good a right to ordain as to administer the Lord's supper.... But I see abundant of reasons why I should not use that right, unless I was turned out of the Church."[25] He called himself a "scriptural episkopos" and acted to assure the future good of the Christianity in America.

The fact that these ordinations were for America is significant. Wesley made it clear that, even though he had been pressured by English Methodists to ordain, he had not done so because the Church of England was the established national church. In America, on the other hand, there was no established church, and he was free to initiate a new church for the continent. The problem in England then, was not theological but legal. Theologically Wesley judged that he was acting as a bishop to the Methodists both in England and in America. In England legal provisions of the established church caused him to refrain from using the prerogative of a bishop to ordain, but no such limitation applied in the case of America:

> For many years I have been importuned from time to time to exercise this right by ordaining part of our travelling preachers. But I have still refused, not only for peace' sake, but because I was determined as little as possible to violate the established order of the National Church to which I belonged.

But the case is widely different between England and North America. Here there are bishops who have a legal jurisdiction: in America there are none, neither any parish ministers. So that for some hundred miles together there is none either to baptize or to administer the Lord's Supper. Here, therefore, my scruples are at an end; and I conceive myself at full liberty, as I violate no order and invade no man's right by appointing and sending labourers into the harvest.[26]

Wesley's actions in ordaining ministers for America, and later for Scotland, Newfoundland, Nova Scotia, the West Indies and ultimately for England (about twenty-five in all), were consistent with his understanding of ministry.

Provision of The Sunday Service Ordinal

The newly appointed Superintendent of American Methodism, Dr. Thomas Coke, arrived in New York on November 3, 1784 along with Vasey and Whatcoat. With him he brought the Articles of Religion for the new church, which were the 39 Articles of the Church of England abridged by Wesley to number 24, a general letter from Wesley to the "Brethren in America," and *The Sunday Service*, based on the 1662 *Book of Common Prayer*, but revised by Wesley for American Methodists. *The Sunday Service* was not only a service for Sunday worship, but it included services for baptism, the Lord's Supper, and other occasional pastoral services such as marriage and burial of the dead. It also provided an ordinal with services for the ordination of deacons, elders, and superintendents.[27] *The Sunday Service* was not used according to Wesley's directive. It was not practical for the new church in the rough frontier of America, but it did provide the ritual for sacramental services, and the ordinal has been used almost exactly as Wesley sent it up to this day. (An optional alternative ordinal was approved for the first time in 1980.) Wesley's ordinal is one of Methodism's most direct links to its founder, and behind Wesley to Catholic Christianity.

In the ordination services Wesley made a number of changes from the liturgy of the Church of England, but the major ingredients are all present. He left the word "deacon" unchanged, but changed "priest" to "elder" and "bishop" to "superintendent." He removed language specifically appropriate to England and the national church, but left the bulk of the rubrics and prayers fundamentally unaltered. Albert Outler has observed that the ordinal "disengaged the office of deacon from its restricted focus in a single parish and made it part of the itinerant ministry."[28] Wesley included the diaconate in the ordained ministries of the new church, perhaps simply because it was traditional in Anglicanism and the Catholic tradition. That deacons were to be itinerant ministers under appointment is significant, however, because it signaled that the diaconate was a part of the plan of Methodist ministry.

Two major conclusions follow from analysis of *The Sunday Service* ordinal:

1. *Wesley clearly intended to establish an independent Methodist Church in America.* The reality of the American Revolution meant that Methodism in America could be different from Methodism in England. The absence of an established church meant that Methodism could be a church. Certainly Wesley had in mind that he would appoint the superintendents, but that it would be a church, and a church different from Methodism in England is clear.

2. *Wesley intended that the church have an episcopal structure.* Wesley was always an episcopalian. When he did take the extraordinary step of ordaining men to ministry himself he did not reject episcopacy and espouse a presbyterial form of ordination. He argued that theologically he was a bishop, a "scriptural episkopos," even though he had not been formally consecrated.[29] Furthermore, if he had not intended for Coke and Asbury to *function* as bishops, though he used the word "superintendent" (which, as we saw in the last chapter, is an appropriate translation of the Greek), he surely would not have "ordained" Coke, who was already an elder, a "superintendent." Wesley sent American Methodism a structure of ministry that included deacons, elders, and superintendents. He also

65

sent his understanding of the meaning of ministerial orders, which included the position that presbyters and bishops are one order, but are functionally different because of the bishop's superintending role. Perhaps the most conclusive evidence for Wesley's intention that the superintendent was to function theologically as a bishop is that the act of ordination itself was reserved for the superintendent. The ordinal calls for the superintendent to lay hands on the deacons and, along with other elders, to ordain elders. Why Wesley did not use the word bishop cannot be answered authoritatively. I think it was because for him the title was identified specifically with Anglican episcopacy and Wesley recoiled from the pomp and circumstance that went with the bishops who were "lords of the realm." He seemed to want for Methodism an episcopal government that would not carry with it those aspects of episcopacy he found objectionable. He intended a "scriptural episkopos."

Continuation of the Apostolic Ministry

What do we make of Wesley's understanding of ministry and the pattern of ministry he left to Methodism? As we have seen, Wesley never developed a clear systematic theological position in regard to ministry or ordination. Our evidence is what he said about what he was doing as he shaped the Methodist movement in England, and established a new church for America.

Wesley's relationship to the Church of England is problematic at best. Insisting that he was always loyal, he nevertheless led a movement that became increasingly separatist. He openly defied its rules when he took upon himself authority to ordain. Charles Wesley maintained that ordination was separation, but John maintained his position to the end. We must face the fact that despite all of Wesley's claims about presbyters and bishops being of the same order, Anglican theology and practice makes what he did wrong in the eyes of the Anglicans. He was never a consecrated bishop. Some Anglican commentators have tried to excuse him by arguing that he was really establishing presbyteral ordination for America, and that his "ordination" of Coke was simply appointment to the role of "leader" of the church in America, as Wesley's personal representative. According to this view, Coke manipulated Wesley so that he could subsequently use the title "bishop."[30] I think this is wrong since the evidence is that Wesley believed in episcopacy and that, even in his old age, he was not manipulated by anyone about important matters. Furthermore, I find no evidence in the correspondence between Coke and Wesley to sustain the view that Coke was merely grasping after preferment. Going to America as Superintendent of Methodism in 1784 was hardly preferment!

We have to content ourselves with the fact that Wesley did not have systematic clarity about the theological or practical implications of the pattern of ministry for Methodists either in England or in America. At first he certainly did not intend to start a church, but events and the mission brought him finally to the point where he did intend to found a church for America. There are, of course, other theological matters where Wesley is systematically vague (or inconsistent). An example is his understanding of baptism and its relationship to justification, regeneration and sanctification. He maintains the truth and power of infant baptism even as he insists on a subsequent experience of new birth and regeneration. He wanted to embrace both Catholic teaching, as mediated in Anglicanism, and the truths he came to know and believe as a result of his evangelical experience.

I suggested at the beginning of this chapter that to understand the Wesleyan conception of ministry it is necessary to begin with the Anglican context. Wesley always assumed the Anglican context, but then added to it the flexibility which derives from the conviction that priority always is given to the actual needs of mission in the world. Wesley believed that the mission of the church was a higher authority than church order. He did not lightly deviate from the authority of church order, but, as we have seen, he did do so on a number of matters.

Let us not make the mistake of simply thinking that pragmatic matters took priority with Wesley. What is at stake are two different theological positions. Wesley was convinced that evangelical mission must be primary rather than church order, even though he was well aware that church order functions to assure the integrity of the gospel for mission.

Wesley did not believe that the integrity of the apostolic ministry was dependent on the unbroken succession of bishops, though he did believe that episcopal order served the church well. Ministry derives from Jesus Christ and is a gift of God through the Holy Spirit and takes place through the ecclesiastical structures of the church, though sometimes mission requires going outside of them. The theological integrity of Christian teaching is related to the faithful living of the community of Jesus Christ. Leadership of the community is a gift from God and is authenticated in mission. Ordination sets persons apart for particular leadership, and it has an essential place in the total ministry of the church. Ordination is one aspect of Wesley's larger understanding of Christian ministry. The apostolic ministry does not depend on any particular structures or polity but finds its expression in the essential character of the evangelical mission of the gospel of Jesus Christ.

Chapter IV
Ordination in American Methodism

... preach the word, be urgent in season and out of season, con-
vince, rebuke and exhort, be unfailing in patience and in
teaching.
                                                    – 2 Timothy 4:1-5

Our consideration of ministry in the Wesleyan tradition has
shown how Wesley arrived at his decision to ordain men for
American Methodism, and how he decided the new church
should be structured. Wesley's decisions, his plan, and his argument for the plan were developed, in the American setting,
into a vigorous episcopal polity in which the theological principles of itineracy, appointment and connection were fundamental. In Britain, because of the Anglican state church, these
same principles were manifest, after Wesley's death, in a non-
episcopal polity. American episcopal Methodism became a
unique church polity, informed by Wesley, but shaped by
Asbury and the American context.

The 1784 Christmas Conference

The Christmas Conference of 1784 is decisive for any consideration of ordination in Methodism. It marks the translation of
Methodist ministerial orders from Wesley to Asbury and
American Methodism. So important were the events of 1784,
both in England and in America, that Bishop John Tigert, writing in 1893, would look back and call it "the grand climacteric

year."[1] The capstone of the "grand climacteric year" was the Christmas Conference.

After Thomas Coke arrived in America with Thomas Vasey and Richard Whatcoat, on November 3, 1784, he met with Francis Asbury, and other leaders of the Methodist movement, to consider Wesley's plan. They determined that a Conference of the preachers was needed, and one was called for Christmas Eve in Baltimore. The Conference met in Lovely Lane Meeting House to explain the plan Wesley had sent with Dr. Coke, and to organize for the future. Of the eighty-one preachers then in America, about sixty were present. The Conference met for ten days, and did much important business, but it did three things of determinative significance specifically in regard to ministry:

1. The Conference organized and named the Methodist Episcopal Church. The importance of the choice of name and organization cannot be over-emphasized. Certainly Wesley sent a plan for an episcopal church structure, but the frontier Americans might have altered the plan. They did not, and in fact, by the choice of name, specifically elected episcopal structure. The Reverend Thomas Ware, who was present at the Christmas Conference, remembered that John Dickens proposed the name Methodist Episcopal Church. Ware wrote, "all agreeing that the plan of general superintendency, which had been adopted, was a species of episcopacy, the motion on Mr. Dickens' suggestion was carried without, I think, a dissenting voice."[2] With the episcopal structure went the adoption of the three ministries of deacons, elders and superintendents (they would soon use the word "bishop"). American Episcopal Methodism has thus from the beginning elected persons to these three offices. Each of the three ordained offices was understood to be part of the itinerant ministry.

2. The Conference elected Francis Asbury to be a general superintendent and he was ordained. Asbury believed that the general superintendent should be elected and, although he was appointed by Wesley, he insisted upon election by the Conference. The tradition of the election of bishops entered American

Methodism by Asbury's decision. He was ordained deacon on Christmas Day, Saturday, December 25, and elder on Sunday, December 26, by Coke, along with Whatcoat and Vasey. His ordination as superintendent came on Monday, December 27, and at this service, Philip William Otterbein, a German Reformed pastor, also laid on hands.

There has been much debate about the change in nomenclature from superintendent to bishop. Wesley used the term superintendent to distinguish the office from that of an Anglican bishop. At the same time, his plan and ordinal clearly called for a "set apart" ministry that would function as an episcopacy; and "superintendent" is an alternative English translation of *episkopos*. The Christmas Conference recognized this when it chose the name of the new church. Coke and Asbury argued that the term "bishop" was more biblical and it certainly fit the intention of the church. The *Discipline* of 1787 introduced the title "bishop," and the Conference of 1792 officially changed "superintendent" to "bishop" in the ordinal.[3]

3. The Conference elected other preachers to the offices of deacon and elder, and they were ordained. After Asbury was ordained, the Conference proceeded to the election of others. The exact numbers are not available, because official minutes do not exist, but about twelve elders and three deacons were elected and ordained, and the rest remained lay preachers. The deacons and elders became part of the itinerant ministry of the new church.

One of the elders was appointed to Antigua, in the Caribbean, two to Nova Scotia, and the rest to the United States.

The Christmas Conference received Wesley's plan and, with slight modification, implemented it for American Methodism. It also received and established ministerial orders for the Methodist Episcopal Church. We need now to consider the nature and function of those orders.

Ministry in American Episcopal Methodism

The lack of systematic clarity about ordination we noticed in John Wesley was bequeathed to American Methodism. Wesley's understanding of the ministry of Methodism best functioned in the Anglican context where it could play the role of a renewal movement. But circumstances made continuation in that role impossible, and the effort to move from a society to a church was particularly difficult in regard to ministry and ordination. Let us first consider the roles of bishops, elders and deacons. These roles were explicated for the first time in the *Form of Discipline for the Ministers, Preachers, and Other Members of the Methodist Episcopal Church in America* adopted by the Christmas Conference, and published in 1785.

The Conference organized the *Discipline* through a series of questions and answers which included consideration of the three offices of ministry. Question 26 asks, "What is the office of a superintendent?" The answer is given as follows:

> To ordain superintendents, elders and deacons; to preside as a moderator in our Conferences; to fix the appointments of the preachers for the several circuits; and, in the intervals of the Conference, to change, receive or suspend preachers, as necessity may require; and to receive appeals from preachers and people and to decide them. N.B. No persons shall be ordained a superintendent, elder, or deacon, without the consent of the majority of the Conference, and the consent and imposition of hands of a superintendent. . . .[4]

Two matters of importance need to be noticed about this earliest description of the Methodist episcopacy. One is that only the bishop may ordain. This is the key to an inconsistency that has plagued episcopal Methodism ever since. On the one hand, following Wesley's judgment that elders and bishops were of one order, we have persisted in asserting that episcopal Methodism has two orders of ordained ministry, namely deacons and elders, but three offices. But, from the beginning, we have structured and treated the episcopacy as a third order. The sole power to ordain, coupled with life tenure, are evidences of the fact that Methodist episcopacy was delegated unique powers, and therefore treated as a third order. Secondly, from the beginning, the bishop was empowered to appoint the ministry. Here American Methodism was completely consistent with Wesley's understanding that ministry is appointed. These two aspects of Methodist episcopacy have been fundamental to the church since its beginning in 1784, while other aspects of the office, for instance the veto power over ordination, has changed. The earliest *Discipline* established a role for the Conference in the process of ordination from the outset. Entry into the ordained Methodist ministry has always required the consent of the Conference as well as the laying on of hands by the bishop and prayer for the gift of the Holy Spirit.

Question 30 asks about the office of an elder; and the answer is:

> To administer the sacraments of baptism and the Lord's supper, and to perform all the other rites prescribed by our Liturgy.

Question 31 inquires about the office of a deacon:

> To baptize in the absence of an elder, to assist the elder in the administration of the Lord's supper, to marry, bury the dead, and read the Liturgy to the people as prescribed, except what relates to the administration of the Lord's supper.[5]

It is clear that only elders are to celebrate the Holy Communion, but deacons are to lead the other services of the church and to assist the elder. These descriptions are essentially the same as those of the Church of England, rooted, of course, in Catholic Christianity. American Methodists adopted for themselves understanding of the role of bishops, elders and deacons such as they had known in England. Only bishops could ordain; celebration of the Eucharist was reserved for elders (or bishops, of course), and deacons did other services of the church, and assisted the elders. This description of ordained ministerial or-

73

ders has remained basically consistent in Methodism. The formal essential understanding of what ordination authorizes one to do is the same today as at the Christmas Conference. American episcopal Methodism took this aspect of its ecclesiology from Anglicanism.

Early American Methodists were consistent with Wesley in their judgment that preaching was not related to ordination. Significantly, the description of the offices of superintendent, elder and deacon make no reference to preaching. This is not surprising in that the impetus to ordain for America was only in regard to sacramental ministries. Furthermore, ordination was not related to a local congregation but was related to traveling. As we saw in chapter II, one of the complaints of the Continental Reformers about Roman Catholic understanding of ordination was that it was not dependent on service in a local congregation but was an "absolute ordination" which gave powers of ordination to the individual priest apart from the faithful community. Methodism's approach was closer to the Catholic view in that ordination was not tied to a local church. Ordination was not done in a local congregation but in the Conference to symbolize that ordained ministry is sent to congregations, and is not dependent on them. This approach emphasized the connectional character of the church.

Methodist ordination was not, however, the "absolute ordination" of Catholicism in that it was tied to the traveling ministry. While the Protestant Reformed Tradition related ordination to service in a local congregation, Methodist ordination was dependent on service in the traveling ministry of the connection. The Discipline adopted by the Christmas Conference makes this clear in regard to bishops:

> Question 28. If the superintendent ceases from traveling at large among the people, shall he exercise his office in any degree? Answer. If he ceases from traveling without the consent of the Conference, he shall not thereafter exercise any ministerial function whatsoever in our Church.

It also makes it clear in regard to elders and deacons:

Question 35. How are we to proceed with those elders or deacons who cease from traveling? Answer. Unless they have the
permission of the Conference declared under the hand of a
superintendent, they are on no account to exercise any of the
peculiar functions of those offices among us. And if they do,
they are to be expelled immediately.[6]

American Methodism coupled Wesley's conviction that the
traveling ministry was essential to Methodism with an episcopal structure and description of the powers of ordination.

The ordained ministry was to be a traveling ministry with
responsibility for the connectional character of the church.
Bishops were general superintendents with obligations for the
entire connection, not just a particular region. Elders might
serve a particular charge, but their concern was not merely
local. This meant, by the way, that from the beginning,
ordained ministers were appointed to connectional work as
well as to local charges. Methodism has always appointed
some elders to what we now call "special appointments."
These appointments were consistent with ordination and
served the connectional needs. The traveling ministry of
episcopal Methodism made possible the deployment of ordained ministry wherever, and for whatever tasks, it was
needed.

American Methodism combined a number of factors to produce its ministry. These included the lay preachers of the
Wesleyan tradition, the episcopal polity sent by Wesley, a pattern of ordination characteristic of Anglicanism, and the idea of
a traveling, connectional ministry. This combination has resulted in a number of built-in tensions.

Perhaps the most obvious tension is that between the ministry of preaching and the ministry of sacramental administration. Among early Methodists preaching was always primary.
Wesley made this clear as he expressed his view of the unique
place of Methodism in the eighteenth century revival. At the
same time, the revival included sacramental observance, and

the need for regular reception of the Holy Communion on the part of Methodists was emphasized by Wesley. Word and sacrament went together. Methodism was famous for its lay preachers, but until very late in Wesley's life, the movement relied on ordained ministers of the Church of England for the essential ministry of the sacraments. Once Wesley ordained ministers for America, however, he introduced a serious tension. The new church would have both lay preachers and ordained preachers, and practically, the lines would sometimes blur.

In principle the idea was sound. The problem was a lack of ordained clergy for sacramental administration. The solution was to ordain some, and combine ordination with full membership in the conference. This introduced another distinction that resulted in tension. Methodism distinguished between the local ministry and the traveling ministry. The local preacher was not ordained and not part of the itinerancy. The ordained minister was a full member of the conference and appointed as a part of the itinerant ministry. The way it worked in the early days of American Methodism was that the traveling elder was appointed to a territory or circuit covering a large geographic area. The local preacher was licensed to preach, and worked to advance the ministry of the church in a specific, local community. The traveling elder would preach, serve as pastor, and celebrate the Holy Communion. This is one of the reasons early Methodists moved away from Wesley's recommendation about weekly Eucharistic celebration. The traveling elder could not be present every week, and so he would serve Communion and baptize at each place on the circuit when he preached. Bishop Asbury preferred an informal, preaching-centered style of worship, and the "traveling plan," with its distinction between ordained traveling elders and unordained local preachers, was to his liking.[7]

The relationship between the traveling elders and local preachers worked both in theory and in practice in the early days, but problems arose as Methodism became more localized when communities and churches grew. After Methodism's traveling ministry developed into a semi-settled ministry, the problems inherent in the system began to grow. Local preachers continued to serve where an elder was not available; but the need for local preachers was diminished as traveling elders became semi-settled. I use the term semi-settled because although the idea of itineracy was still very much alive, the elders would be appointed to one place for a year or two and eventually for longer periods. Because Methodism did not have a tradition of weekly Communion, however, even after elders were settled and could have celebrated the sacrament in the congregation every week, neither they nor the people thought they should. At first quarterly Communion was practiced out of necessity because it was the only time the traveling elder was present. Later they practiced it because they knew no better, and thought that was the way it ought to be.

The semi-settlement of the traveling elders and the changed circumstances of the local preachers, coupled with the infrequent, perhaps quarterly, sacramental celebrations, meant that the unique identity of the traveling elder was threatened, if not lost. That unique identity had to do with itineracy, sacramental ministry, and conference membership. When the elder was semi-settled, and when the sacraments were not central, the untutored eye could not tell the local preacher and the traveling elder apart, except that one was a full member of the annual conference and the other was not. But that distinction did not mean much, if anything, to laity.

Local preachers would actually serve congregations, and care for them with great effectiveness, in much the same way as would a traveling elder. The term "preacher in charge" was used to refer to the person appointed by the bishop to have pastoral responsibility for a "charge," which could be a circuit, station or mission. Early in the nineteenth century, the *Discipline* began to indicate that the "preacher in charge" might be an elder, deacon or "preacher." Because Holy Communion was not central to the life of the congregations, and because Methodism made the distinction between the preaching ministry and the ordained ministry, the church developed a pattern in which many local congregations were served by unordained preachers.

77

The pressure then mounted, both on the part of the local congregations, and on the part of the local preachers, to let local pastors serve Holy Communion in their charges. On the grounds that these persons were serving specific appointments under the direct supervision of the Presiding Elder (what we now call a District Superintendent), Methodism allowed the local preacher to administer the sacraments only in that specific charge. This appeared formally for the first time in *The Doctrines and Discipline of the Methodist Episcopal Church, South* in 1926. Among the duties of the preacher in charge were: "To preach the gospel; to celebrate the rite of matrimony, ...in the absence of an elder or Bishop, to administer baptism and the sacrament of the Lord's Supper with the understanding that no permanent powers of ordination are conferred until granted by the laying on of hands. . . ."[8] This description appears in each successive *Discipline of the Methodist Episcopal Church, South* until the reunion of 1939.

The Methodist Episcopal Church did not allow unordained local preachers to celebrate Holy Communion, but it did permit Baptism: "Unordained Local Preachers, only while serving as regularly appointed Pastors of Charges, shall be authorized to administer the rite of Baptism, and when the laws of the State permit, to solemnize Matrimony. . . ."[9] At the time of the merger in 1939, the more lenient approach prevailed, and The Methodist Church allowed unordained local preachers to administer the sacraments in their own charges:

> Unordained Local Preachers, only while serving as regularly appointed Pastors of charges, shall be authorized to administer the Sacraments of Baptism and of the Lord's Supper. . . .[10]

This provision remained in the *Discipline* in basically this form from the Uniting Conference in 1939 to 1968, when The Methodist Church and the Evangelical United Brethren joined to become The United Methodist Church. Even so, there was ambivalence about the situation. Those leaders of the church who were concerned about the history and theology of ministry recognized the confusion and inconsistency.

During the 1960-64 quadrennium The Methodist Church appointed a Study Committee on the Ministry. Its report made sweeping proposals for change, including a prohibition against unordained ministers administering the sacraments.[11] The Report was not adopted. The failure of General Conference to accept the Commission's recommendations is indicative of the caution which has characterized church response to every proposal to change the traditional pattern of ministry originally adopted in 1784. The provision allowing local preachers to administer the sacraments, however, not only was not part of the tradition, but contradicted it. The 1968 merger of The Methodist Church with the Evangelical United Brethren was the occasion to rescind permission for unordained pastors to administer the sacraments.[12] But by 1976 the church reversed itself again because of the practical problems which resulted in the many charges served by local pastors.[13] Currently local pastors are allowed to administer the sacraments "while assigned to a particular charge."[14]

The confusing provision made by Methodism to allow unordained pastors to administer the sacraments is at once inconsistent with Wesley and consistent with American Methodism's appropriation of the Wesleyan tradition. The inconsistency is clear. Wesley's extraordinary ordinations were done precisely to avoid administration without ordination. The consistency is that American Methodism emphasized the Wesleyan concern for flexibility in the face of practical need, as well as that for sacramental ministries. Local congregations wanted their own pastors to celebrate the sacraments.

The problems with ordination demonstrate as well as anything that American episcopal Methodism was a "new creation," not simply Wesley's Methodism in America. Methodism in the United States became a large, popular movement. It set rigorous standards for its ordained ministry, and yet it was also aggressively evangelistic and had more congregations to supply with leadership than it had ordained ministers in full connection. The move to allow local preachers to administer the sacraments in their specific charges was pragmatic, pastorally sensitive and missional; but it was also confused and theologically wrong.

One alternative would have been to break the equation of ordination with full membership in the annual conference and guaranteed appointment, but that was never proposed. The other alternative was to refuse to let local preachers celebrate the sacraments and make other provisions for the sacraments, but when this was tried, the practical problems for a large and popular church were formidable. In the course of its development, American Methodism gradually changed its practice in regard to its traditional understanding of ordained ministry and lay ministry. The result was confusion. This confusion, the result of a problematic ecclesiology, is the reason a vital theology of ordination has been absent from American Methodism.

I began the first chapter of this book by observing that, on the whole, Methodists have not paid a great deal of attention to ordination. Now we see why this is so; by the twentieth century, the long-held Methodist view that no administration of the sacraments was possible apart from ordination, which was Wesley's only reason for ordaining for America, was changed to accommodate changed conditions. The integrity of ordination was undercut because the fine points of theology were not determinative for American Methodists. The church could not explain with clarity the meaning of ordination because it had deviated from its own tradition in the matter.

Perhaps it would be more accurate to say that what happened was that the theology and practice of ordination was displaced by another aspect of the tradition, namely the priority of mission, and particularly that aspect of mission which was the highest priority for nineteenth-century Methodism, evangelism. The major work of the early American Methodist preacher was evangelism.[15] The chief end of preaching was conversion and the church grew rapidly. Sacramental ministries, pastoral care, teaching and administration all were subordinate to evangelism. Ordination seemed almost incidental. The fact that the ordinal was changed hardly at all from the initial service sent by Wesley until 1980, when General Conference, without replacing the original, approved an alternate service, might indicate that ordination did not matter a great deal to most Methodists, as much as it might indicate reverence for Wesley's original text. Ordination came to mean little more than authorization for ministry and full membership in the annual conference. Only in recent years, for the reasons I noted in Chapter One, have we been forced to look with new eyes at the meaning of ordination.

Diversity and Unity in the Tradition

Thus far in this chapter we have examined episcopal Methodism, which was the dominant tradition in America. Mention must be made, however, of other branches of the Wesleyan tradition which dealt with ministry, and ordination, in a different way. In 1830 a group of dissenters from episcopal Methodism broke away to form the Methodist Protestant Church. At their organizing General Conference they eliminated episcopacy and replaced the bishop with an annual conference president. Although democratic and populist, Methodist Protestantism did not reject ordination, which remained tied to annual conference membership and administration of the sacraments. It was, however, a presbyteral ordination in which no episcopal hands were required. When the Methodist Protestant Church merged with the Methodist Episcopal Church and the Methodist Episcopal Church, South, in 1939, to form The Methodist Church, the understanding and order of ministry which had informed Episcopal Methodism since 1784 prevailed in the new united Methodism.

The Evangelical United Brethren Church, which merged with The Methodist Church in 1968 to form The United Methodist Church, traced its roots to the former Evangelical Church and the United Brethren Church. These groups originated under the leadership of Jacob Albright and Philip William Otterbein, respectively. The Evangelical United Brethren were structured and functioned much as Methodists, but in regard to ministry, they recognized one ordained order, which they called elders, although they also had bishops. The E.U.B. bishops were different from Methodist bishops, however, in that they had terms rather than life tenure, and therefore the functional character of the office was more apparent. At the time of the merger in 1968, the historic tradition of episcopal Methodism was adopted by The United Methodist Church, including the three offices of deacon, elders and bishops. Provisions for the retirement of active bishops was made, but bishops were to serve for life, and would be called upon for leadership to exercise the episcopal office in times of need. Episcopal office and responsibilities do not end at retirement from active service.

World-wide Methodism, as represented in the World Methodist Council, includes a number of diverse traditions in regard to the structure of ministry. The Wesleyan-Methodist understanding of ministry does not depend on one specific structure for its authenticity or integrity. That all churches in the Wesleyan tradition recognize this fact and function according to Wesley's conception of ordained ministry is evidenced by the mutual recognition of ministerial orders. Episcopal Methodism is the dominant American Methodist tradition, however. In addition to United Methodism, it includes the historic black Methodist denominations, the African Methodist Episcopal Church, the African Methodist Episcopal Zion Church and the Christian Methodist Episcopal Church.

The Continuity of Ordination

We have seen that confusion about the theology of ordination produced tensions in American Methodism's understanding of ministry. Moreover our wider study demonstrates that the diversity characteristic of Methodism is also present in the larger Christian community. The history of all traditions within Christianity manifest diversity in regard to the theology and practice of ordination. There are, however, certain points of continuity which can be identified as central to consideration of ordination in Methodism.

1. Ordination is the way Methodism sets some apart for sacramental ministries. Throughout its history Methodism has

linked ordination and sacramental ministries. Wesley's distinction between authorization for preaching and for sacramental ministries was carried over into later Methodism. The theological conviction that there is to be no administration of the sacraments without ordination led Wesley to his decision to act as a "scriptural episkopos" in the "extraordinary" ordinations for America. Even when Methodism took the step of allowing unordained preachers to administer the sacraments only in the charge to which they were appointed, it was recognized to be exceptional. The continued debate demonstrates that it is problematic because it contradicts the Wesleyan tradition.

2. Ordination includes vows which make the ordinand accountable to the church. These vows bind the ordinand, and to this extent, and in this way, the ordinand is a different person as a result of ordination. Through the laying on of hands, and the prayer for the imposition of the gift and grace of the Holy Spirit, the ordained person is "set apart" by and for the church. Through a complex process involving God's call and the call of the church, the annual conference and the ordinand enter into mutual covenants. The person who is ordained takes vows in which he or she freely takes the yoke of obedience. These are the questions to which every person ordained must freely respond affirmatively:

Are you persuaded that the Holy Scriptures contain all truth required for eternal salvation through faith in Jesus Christ? And are you determined out of the same Holy Scriptures so to instruct the people committed to your charge that they may enter into eternal life?

Will you give faithful diligence duly to minister the doctrine of Christ, the Sacraments, and the discipline of the Church, and in the spirit of Christ to defend the Church against all doctrine contrary to God's Word?

Will you be diligent in prayer, in the reading of the Holy Scriptures, and in such studies as help to the knowledge of God and of his kingdom?

Will you apply all your diligence to frame and fashion your own lives and the lives of your families according to the teachings of Christ?

Will you maintain and set forward, as much as lieth in you, quietness, peace, and love among all Christian people, and especially among them that shall be committed to your charge?

Will you reverently heed them to whom the charge over you is committed, following with a glad mind and will their godly admonitions?[16]

The vows of ordination are serious. They represent a willing surrender of the self to God and the church in a very specific way. Methodism has never believed that ordination imparts a permanent character which gives one unique powers. But neither is it the case that Methodism has believed that ordination results in no change in the ordinand. There is a change. The change is the result of one's commitment to subordinate the self to the needs of the total ministry of the church, and the fact that one is set apart for the unique responsibility of ministering to God's people through sacramental celebration.

The ordained person has officially yielded to the church a role in his or her self-definition. In part, this is what we mean when we say that ordained ministry makes one a "representative person." The ordained minister by definition is tied to the church and its ministry.

3. Methodists understand the true church to be connectional, not local, therefore ordination is a connectional reality and not dependent on any specific congregation. Because it is related to the traveling ministry, ordination also confers a lifelong role in the church which one carries wherever one serves in ministry. Ordination is not limited to a specific annual conference but is genuinely connectional.

4. Ordained ministers in Methodism are itinerants who are appointed and sent. The Methodist itineracy varies in different settings and times, but the theological idea is that ministry is not local. Ordained ministry is sent to congregations not called by them. The pastor is not dependent upon local customs or prejudices, but is freed for the fullness of ministry in a specific place. The total church is assured that ordained ministry can be placed according to particular needs in the context of wholeness.

American Methodism has always struggled with the tension between being primarily an evangelical society seeking converts to the gospel of Jesus Christ and a church established to serve the pastoral needs of Christian believers. Seeking to be true to Wesley, Methodists wanted to have it both ways. Theological convictions about evangelism and personal and social reform were tied to convictions about Methodism's obligations to nurture its people and assist in the development of the nation. The urge to respond to pressing missional needs militated against exactitude in theology and polity, but from 1784 on, Methodism was also destined to play the sociological role of a church for the new nation. This role required the trappings of a church, including an ordained ministry fulfilling the whole range of pastoral responsibilities. Ordination is a good case study because it illustrates these tensions and reminds us that, for Methodism, the church of Jesus Christ always exists as a dynamic community between continuity, as mediated in Scripture and tradition, and the reality of God's present activity, as mediated in the experience of the Holy Spirit.

Chapter V
The Meaning of Ordination

Do not neglect the gift you have, which was given you by prophetic utterance when the elders laid their hands upon you.
— 1 Timothy 4:14

We began this study of ordination in Methodism by attend-
ing to the ministry of the whole people of God. We have seen
that all Christians are called to ministry, and that Baptism, as
the sacrament of initiation into the church, is also a commis-
sioning for ministry. The church has always set aside some
persons for the tasks of ordained ministry, however, and we
have traced how ordination developed in Christianity and
specifically in Methodism. No one pattern of ministry exists in
ecumenical Christianity, and within Methodism there is diversity, though certain continuities inform all considerations of
ordination in the Wesleyan tradition. In this chapter we will
look systematically at the theological issues which must be
dealt with if the meaning of ordination is to be understood.

The Vocation to Ordained Ministry

Usually entry into ordained ministry begins with the perception of a call to a person's inner self from God. The exact
nature of God's inner call cannot easily be articulated. It comes
in different ways to different people. For some it may be

gradual and low-key; for others it may occur at a specific time and be dramatic.

The recognition of inner call is an essential part of the vocation for ordained ministry. This, as we have seen, was one of John Wesley's strong convictions. He called it the "inward call." If one is not convinced through inner experience of God's call, then the spiritual resources will not be present for effective ministry. The work of the Holy Spirit in leading persons to ordination is not capricious, and the inner call is compatible with one's gifts and graces for ministry in the church.

It is not enough to sense the reality of the inner call. Sometimes persons may misperceive the nature of inner experience. Consideration of ordained ministry is complex because there is a necessary second component. This is the call of God which comes from and through the church. Wesley called this the "outward call." Some persons are recognized by the church as having the abilities necessary for effectiveness in ordained ministry. Unless one is recognized as having these gifts, one will not be able to function in service to church and world as an ordained minister.

The two aspects of the call to ordained ministry, the "inner call" and the "outward call," do not always or necessarily occur in a particular order. The church may recognize a call in us that we do not recognize. The "church's call" may precede the "inner call." I talked with a pastor not long ago who told me that he would not be in ordained ministry except for a woman in the local church where he previously had been a lay member. She confronted him with her observation that God might be calling him to ordination. The thought and prayer that followed allowed him to recognize and affirm his call.

This is the theological grounding for talking to men and women about ordained ministry. It is not that we are recruiting, as if ministry were one career option among others, but it is that we are encouraging serious Christian persons to be open to the possibility that they might be called. The leadership of God's people is not an individual thing; one cannot be a "solo practitioner." The Christian community may recognize gifts and graces in one for ordained ministry even when the individual may not recognize them. God works through the church to provide ministry for the church and for the world.

Some pastors and congregations are particularly effective at recognizing and encouraging gifts and graces for ordained ministry. There are certain pastors who make a special effort to cultivate persons and follow them through seminary into leadership of the church. There are some congregations who nurture persons in such a way that they are able to recognize the vocation to ordination. Perhaps the key to this vital work is the conviction that a major obligation of the Christian community is the development of leadership, through the grace of God, for the future.

The Role of the Church

As our historical survey demonstrates, ordination has always been an act of the church as well as God's act in the church. This means that the church establishes qualifications and a process by which judgment can be made about individual candidates. The role of the church has to do with the "outward call." One may think that he or she has gifts and graces for ministry, but individual judgment is only one aspect of the total process of preparation for ordination. The church must evaluate, judge and confirm the individual's conviction. In this book we have seen that ordination is not a "right." The fact that no person has the "right" to be ordained cannot be overemphasized. The issue is not whether or not a person wants to be a pastor, but whether or not the community wants a person to be ordained. A person's "gifts, graces and promise of future usefulness" must be "observable to the community."[1] The church's ordained ministry is set apart according to the community's judgment about a candidate's suitability.

The process begins with what United Methodism calls "candidacy." Through the use of written materials provided by the church, and consultation with a pastor, men and women who think they may be called explore the meaning of ordination, the implications of servant ministry, and the church's requirements for annual conference membership. The process continues in the local congregation. It is here that persons are best known for their fidelity and abilities. Sometimes local churches are too unreflective about their role in the process. Because they have not been trained to think about the nature of vocation, lay persons are often mystified by a candidate's claim to have a "call to preach." All Christians need to think about the dynamics of vocation to ordained ministry because it is the job of the local congregation to evaluate critically candidates who present themselves. In Methodism no person can advance to the district committee or annual conference board of ministry without the endorsement of the local church. This comes through a meeting of the Charge Conference. These endorsements should never be *pro forma*. Lay committees have responsibility to do serious examination of the candidate and to give careful attention to the candidate's natural and acquired abilities. All of this needs to be done in the context of prayer for the guidance of the Holy Spirit.

The endorsement of the local congregation is not sufficient, however, because ordination is not a local reality. Ordination is done for the whole church, and therefore deliberations on the part of the larger church are necessary. One of the church's most solemn responsibilities is to order its life to judge the adequacy of persons who are candidates for ordained ministry. United Methodism has district committees and annual conference boards who work with candidates. The annual conference board makes a recommendation to the executive session of the clergy at the annual conference. Only ordained elders vote to admit candidates to full membership in the annual conference and to elders orders. This takes place at an executive session of the members in full connection. The 1784 Christmas Conference established that no person could be ordained without the consent of the conference. Originally bishops had a veto power, but in later Methodism this power was removed from the *Discipline*. Currently the annual conference approves candidates and the bishop ordains them.

The reason only ordained elders vote on ordination does not have to do with professional privilege, but with discipline and obligation. Ordination is about responsibility and accountability for the unity of Christianity in regard to essential matters of faith and order. Ordained persons are set apart to assure continuity with the apostolic faith. The yoke of obedience includes commitment to assure fidelity to the gospel in all of its aspects through teaching and example. This requires the discipline, knowledge and commitment which the church demands of its clergy. Ordained ministers are bound to each other, and to the conference, in mutual covenant. This covenant includes expectations about moral character because the way one lives communicates the gospel. Approval of candidates for ordination is one way the church cares for continuity in the fullness of the essential teachings of the Christian gospel. Ordained clergy are successors to the apostles in that they are responsible for maintaining and propagating the apostolic faith. The bonds of covenant obligation require that only those in this relationship vote on ordination.

Qualifications for Ordination

The idea that the church establishes qualifications for its representative officials obviously is not new. Within the canonical books of the New Testament we see evidence that even within the first century A.D. qualifications were established for bishops, deacons and presbyters.[2] Ordination belongs to the church and therefore the church establishes expectations. These can take many forms, but the point is that the church sets standards by which candidates for ordination are judged. Some of these standards are as old as the church itself, some vary in regard to time and place. Standards and qualifications for ordination evidence both continuity and change.

The early church set standards concerning maturity, experience in the faith, knowledge, character, capacity to serve as an example, and natural abilities to lead. Persons too young in years, or young in the faith, were prohibited from ordination until they attained maturity as evidenced to the community. The character of candidates was essential because clergy were to serve as examples to the church and to the world. As leaders they had to be trusted to say and do the "right thing," in Christian terms, even under the duress of persecution. Knowledge of the faith was essential because the clergy were the teachers of the church helping the community to live in such a way that its common life became proclamation of the gospel. Leadership abilities included natural and developed gifts for articulate speech, effective public reading, graceful presence at the Lord's table, service as a spiritual guide, and learning the biblical, historical and theological material essential to ministry. These qualifications have remained constant in some form in most times and places in the life of the church.

There are other standards which have varied in the history of the church according to interpretation in specific settings and times of the church's life. Celibacy is an example of a standard which is not absolute. The scriptures are plain that celibacy was not mandated for leadership in the early church. Roman Catholicism developed a tradition of celibacy for all ordained clergy. Eastern Orthodoxy makes allowance for marriage if it is initiated prior to ordination as a presbyter, but further distinguishes between priests and bishops. Bishops must be celibate. Protestantism has largely approved of marriage for clergy, and at times made it almost mandatory. Wesley, though he married late in life, evidenced a style of ministry best suited to celibacy, and Bishop Asbury, who never married, was explicit in his strong preference that Methodist preachers remain celibate. Ecumenical Christianity deals with clergy marriage in a variety of ways.

For generations the church did not ordain women. Christians interpreted scripture in such a way as to exclude women from ordained leadership, though increasingly scholars came to admit that the prohibition was more traditional than scriptural. Churches in the Catholic tradition continue this prohibition, as do most fundamentalist Protestants. Many Protestant churches judge that God and the church calls women into ordained ministry. The Methodist Church first ordained women in 1956 when the following sentence was included in the Discipline: "Both men and women are included in all provisions of the Discipline which refer to the ministry."[3] Since 1956, Methodism has incorporated women in every aspect of ordained ministry and has demonstrated how change in thinking about qualifications can be manifest in practice.

Sometimes the church will deviate from a standard for theological reasons. An example of this is that in 1984 the Church of Scotland was faced with a candidate for ordained ministry who had killed his mother. Traditionally, guilt of homicide has been a universal impediment to ordination as a Christian minister. The candidate had been through extensive training, counseling and the full process of candidacy, including local church internship. Affirming the power of the forgiveness of God and the obligation of the Christian community to offer forgiveness to a penitent sinner, the Assembly voted that he was eligible for Holy Orders.

In some Christian churches today, including United Methodism, the question of sexual orientation has arisen in regard to standards for ordination. In particular this concerns the ordination of self-professed homosexual persons. The church's discussion of human sexuality, however, should not in the first place be in the context of ordination, but in regard to the larger question of responsible Christian expression of human sexuality. This study has shown that there is a relationship between qualifications for ordination and the way in which the ordained person lives as a "representative figure." In this case the issue is not one's sexual identity, but the way in which one exercises God's gift of human sexuality. Irresponsible exercise of human sexuality is obviously not limited to homosexuals. It is likely that United Methodism today has greater problems with irresponsible heterosexual clergy than with homosexuality. This book cannot attempt a systematic examination of the question of Christian response to human sexuality. Nevertheless, because the issue of ordination and homosexuality has arisen, some observations need to be made.

Contemporary research into homosexuality has called into question the traditional notion that homosexuality is a matter of choice. Biological and psychological analysis suggests that some persons may be genetically formed as sexual persons who are attracted to the same sex. Most persons seem to find their sexual identity as a given fact. Research shows that the matter is very complex however, because there are some persons whose learned response may be significant. It also seems to be the case that there are degrees of homosexuality. Human sexual response is enormously complex and simple answers are not to be found. It will not do for the church to make pronouncements about homosexuality on the basis of simplistic ideas that sexual preference is merely a matter of individual choice and therefore of a person's free will. It does not follow, however, that the church should therefore endorse the practice of homosexuality. Whether one is heterosexual or homosexual, one has the obligation and freedom to act responsibly in accord with Christian teaching. The church does need to learn as much as possible about homosexuality and, in light of additional research and study, it should constantly review its teachings in order to provide appropriate and sensitive guidelines. It is essential that church teaching be accountable to the norms of scripture and tradition as it uses reason to attend to the experience of contemporary reality.[4]

In regard to ordination, the question is whether the candidate will abide by and teach what the church determines to be its understanding of responsible practice of human sexuality. This gets the discussion away from matters of sexual identity to the proper issue of how one lives responsibly as a representative person for and of the community of Jesus Christ. This is applicable to all candidates who seek to serve the church. Our interest in responsible expression of human sexuality must not be limited to considerations of homosexuality.

Scripture and church tradition have been, and are currently understood by the vast majority of Christian churches to offer two alternative ways by which believers are authorized to express human sexuality, celibacy and heterosexual marriage. Sometimes Christians deviate from these guidelines, but this teaching represents the dominant tradition within Christianity. This is the position of United Methodism, which expresses the options as "fidelity in marriage and celibacy in singleness."[5] As this applies to ordination, the question is one's willingness to teach and exemplify the teaching of the church. The issue is not the ordination of homosexual persons, but the responsibility of all ordained persons, as "representative ministers," to abide by the teachings of the church. Ordained persons take upon themselves the yoke of obedience.

The role of the church in ordination is to establish qualifications, nurture candidates, judge the acceptability of candidates in light of established qualifications, and ordain those approved. The church authorizes some persons to do these tasks on its behalf. In United Methodism, the General Conference sets standards for the whole denomination, and annual conferences may add to them. Then local churches, district committees, annual conference boards and the clergy of the conference must make decisions about their application in specific individuals. Authorized persons pray for the guidance of the Holy Spirit and then decide. They may make mistakes – the church is human as well as it is divine – but decisions must be made about candidates for ordination.

The Nature of Ordination

Ordination is God's act in the church. In the laying on of hands with prayer, the gift of the Holy Spirit sets the ordinand apart for the service of leadership in the faith community. Credentialing and authorizing are done in other ways; ordination is a theological reality in which the church asserts its trust that God will give the ordinand grace for the specific ministries of Word, sacrament and order. Although United Methodists do not recognize ordination as a sacrament, it is right to recognize its sacramental qualities. Since its beginning in 1784, American episcopal Methodism has ordained at conference to emphasize that ordination is done for the whole church, and that it includes commitment to itinerancy and appointment. Through the grace of God, the community raises up its ministry, but the ordained also exercise authority over the community. The elder's membership in the annual conference rather than in the local church is a theological affirmation that for Methodists the authority of the appointed pastor does not derive from the local congregation.

THE MEANING OF ORDINATION

Because ordination is God's act in the church, like Baptism, it should be done one time and never repeated. This is because the authenticity of the church and its ministry derives from, and is attested by, the Holy Spirit. Methodism has never believed that there is only one true pattern of church order although there is one true holy and apostolic church. Therefore the validity of ordination has to do with the validity of the church, which may manifest itself in numerous ways but is always attested to by faithful preaching, the administration of the sacraments and holy living. Standards and qualifications for full membership in an annual conference must be rigorously applied to persons coming from other Christian denominations, but persons who hold ministerial orders in other churches should not be ordained again anymore than Methodist ministers who join another church should be reordained. The authenticity of ministerial orders is, unfortunately, one of the most divisive issues in Christianity. The theological question at stake concerns the nature of the church and the way in which God works in the world. Methodists, following Wesley, trust God's grace to shape the church, and think therefore that discussions of "validity" of ministerial orders are less helpful than considerations of the way Christian community recognizes and authenticates the continuity of the apostolic faith through its evangelical witness, holy living and reforming zeal.

Ordination marks us for life. This marking is not a life-long indelible character change, but it is a permanently significant reality. The church perceives the ordained person as different and so does the world. Sometimes this marking is recognized and expressed in simple ways such as the effort to "clean up the language around the preacher," or the perception that even if one enters another vocation and ceases to serve the church as a pastor, one is "different" for having once been a minister. An acquaintance who left the ministry and now wants absolutely no clerical identity commented angrily to me that the image nevertheless "dogs" him wherever he goes. These examples suggest that ministerial identity is different from that of other vocations. The reason for this is that the idea of ordination is to "set apart." Rightly understood, ordination involves commitment freely to relinquish the self in order to become a servant of the church. The self-relinquishing reality of ordination includes the matter of identity. The identity of the ordained is permanently linked to the identity of the church. The ordained are shaped by the church just as they shape the church.

In recent years there has been debate in Methodism about the three ministerial offices. Proposals have come to General Conference to have but one order of ministry and two offices, elders and bishops. In this scheme the diaconate would no longer be a "stepping stone" to elders orders, with a probationary period in between, but would become an office in its own right. Discussions about the permanent diaconate are not limited to Methodism. Roman Catholics and Anglicans are also engaged in exploration toward greater theological clarity.

This study has shown that the Wesleyan tradition includes churches with various ways of ordering ministry. Episcopal Methodism has never insisted that its structure was uniquely right. Nevertheless, since 1784, episcopal Methodism has not deviated from its inherited orders, and caution needs to be exercised on so important a matter. Change is not theologically wrong, but a rejection of the tradition of episcopal Methodism deserves careful examination of our history, theology and ecumenical relations. There are theological constants to authentic ministry in the Wesleyan tradition. These include connection, itineracy and appointment. In the establishment of American episcopal Methodism in 1784, deacons became part of the traveling ministry and were appointed by the bishop, as were elders. Deviation from these principles would be departure from the Wesleyan understanding of ministry. Furthermore, Methodism does not deal with the theology of ministry and ordination in a vacuum. Other traditions are also endeavoring to understand their theological roots and to order ministry for the present time. Methodist reflection needs to take place in an ecumenical context.

In this chapter we have considered the vocation to ordained ministry, qualifications and standards, the role of the church and the nature of ordination. The central idea throughout has been that ordination involves relinquishment of the self to God and the Church of Jesus Christ. Ordained men and women are marked as persons whose lives are defined by service, and whose commitment to God and God's world takes precedence over self-interest. Because ordained persons are human, sin abounds, and the ideal is never fully realized; but authentic ministry demands that the intention must always be genuine. "We are no longer our own, but thine."

Chapter VI
The Representative Character of Ordained Ministers

Tend the flock of God that is your charge, not by constraint, but willingly, not for shameful gain but eagerly, not as domineering over those in your charge, but being examples to the flock.

–1 Peter 5:1-4

One of the major issues facing the ordained ministry is that of identity. The pastor constantly must deal with his or her self-understanding as lay persons, other clergy, the church, and the society impose conceptions of the nature and purpose of the ministerial role. Identity is complex because ordination involves the willingness to take upon oneself the burden of permitting the church to participate in definition of the self. Once ordination has taken place, one is accountable to the church in all things; ordination makes one a representative figure.

In the words of Peter Taylor Forsyth, the ordained ministry "is sacramental to the church as the church itself is sacramental to the world."[1] Ordained persons are representative of Christ. The church recognizes several aspects of Christ's ministry as roles which are combined in ordained ministry. These include the roles of prophet, priest and king. The service of the ordained woman or man incorporates each of these roles through ministries of Word, sacrament and order.

The prophetic role includes teaching and preaching the Word of God and helping the faithful community to live according to the gospel, applying it to personal and corporate life in the world. The prophetic role challenges the church to account for its life in light of the gospel of Jesus Christ. Assisted by the leadership of the ordained, the church itself may play a prophetic role in the larger community. It does this by living as a prophetic community witnessing to the truth of Jesus Christ in mission to the world.

The priestly role embodies Christ's ministry of connection between God and humanity. By becoming human in Jesus, God accepted all of our human frailty and sin, and so freed us from unending guilt, separation and death. We receive God's gifts, chiefly the gift of Christ through the Holy Spirit, and give to God our thanks and praise in total life. This is the dynamic process of justification and sanctification. Responding through faith to God's gift, we seek to live in the light of Christ and the church in turn becomes a priestly people as a community of God's people in the world. This reality is embodied in the sacramental life of the church, in which the truth and reality of the gospel are expressed in their fullness. Through leadership in the essential sacramental ministries of God, the ordained minister exemplifies the priestly role.

Christ's kingly role, the "royal" role, reminds us that the church is of God and is therefore to be shaped according to God's will. The royal role of governor, or rector, exemplifies the fact that ordained ministry is sent to the church to order its life. There is a sense in which the ordained person stands "over against" the community as its "orderer" on behalf of God. The authority for teaching and guiding the faithful community derives from Christ's royal role. The pastoral role includes each of the three aspects of ministerial office, prophetic, priestly and royal, as the one who seeks, through the grace of God, to embody and carry out these multiple tasks is in ministry.

The wholeness of Christian ministry results from the fact that these various roles are united and informed by servant-hood, of which Christ is the chief exemplar. The normative characteristic of all ordained Christian ministry is servant-hood. The one in whose name Christian ministry is done did not seek to be exalted, but he emptied himself and gave his life

99

for others. An ordained minister is a representative figure embodying servanthood.

A representative figure is one in whom the self-as-self becomes secondary. I remember a time when I was called to the home of a parishioner who had died. A physician, the son and brother of clergymen, was in my study when the call came. "Remember," he said, "they don't want you as a friend, but as a pastor." His comment was both true and profound. What was important to them was that I represented the gospel of Jesus Christ and the community of the church.[2] Among the lessons clergy must learn is that they are representative persons for God and God's church. They are "officially" representative figures because that is the nature of the "office" to which they have been called by God and the church.

Servant Leadership

Jesus "came not to be served but to serve, and to give his life as a ransom for many" (Mark 10:45). The leadership of the church is to be a servant leadership. Leadership exists not for itself, but to enable the mission of the Christian community. The stole worn by ordained elders is a liturgical symbol of the towel Jesus used to wash the feet of the disciples at their last supper together. Jesus said, "For I have given you an example, that you should do as I have done to you. Truly, truly, I say to you, a servant is not greater than his master; nor is he who is sent greater than he who sent him" (John 13:15-16).

The idea of servant leadership has been sensitively developed by Robert Greenleaf, as a result of his wide experience in profit and non-profit institutions.[3] Greenleaf's work shows that servant leadership works in a variety of contexts, but is fundamental to the church. The key to the idea is that the leader must allow the mission of the community to be uppermost. Effective leadership results when those being led perceive that the leader is not advancing his or her own ideas or interests, but those of the community. In the case of the church, this means the commands of the gospel.

Servant leadership does not underestimate the essential need for leadership. Warren Bennis, a thoughtful observer of institutions and leadership says that American organizations are "overmanaged and underled."[4] I think this is true of the church. Recent decades have brought to the fore an approach to leadership which emphasizes management. Our church communities have become complex institutions which can absorb enormous amounts of time and energy to keep the operations going. Leadership requires the ability and willingness to step back and think about the reasons for which we exist and the purposes we are supposed to be serving. The church is crying out for insightful leadership in local communities struggling to be faithful, creative and effective servants of Jesus Christ. Pastors must be more than managers.

The kind of leadership we need is that which can help the Christian community to understand its mission and to engage in significant work on behalf of Christ. Sometimes ordained ministers shrink from leadership because they think it is contrary to the humility and self-giving characteristics of Jesus. Sometimes ordained ministers embrace the leadership role to the opposite extreme setting themselves forward with overwhelming ego. Authentic leadership is assertive, but does not advance the self-as-self. The style of servant leadership demanded of ordained ministers is like that described by the Chinese philosopher Lao-Tzu in the sixth century B.C. "At the end of the days of the truly great leader, the people will say about him, 'We did it ourselves.'"

Servant leadership requires the capacity to appreciate and identify with the people served. One of the hallmarks of the early American Methodist circuit riders was their ability to relate effectively to common people and communicate the gospel in terms they could understand. The church struggles to prepare its ministry without alienating the ordained from the people they are called to serve. The process of education and preparation for ordination almost inevitably removes candidates from the settings in which the initial calls to ministry took place, and introduces them to a life style of study and reflection. It can be difficult to go back. Joseph Blenkinsopp makes this observation in regard to the Roman Catholic priesthood: "A priest of working-class origin, . . . soon finds himself 'out of his class,' living at a considerably higher cultural and economic level than what he was accustomed to previously and perhaps eventually becoming estranged from those among whom he grew up."[5] This reality is present in all education because, by definition, education is designed to expose one to new ideas and thus engender a certain alienation from previous experience. The problem is particularly acute for theological education since its purpose is to send graduates back to their communities of origin as servant leaders. The tension is very real because the level of education required of clergy, and the settings in which the education takes place, will often put candidates "out of their class." The complex expectations placed on prospective clergy sometimes makes the ordained ministry seem like other professions, and attitudes develop which are incompatible with the expectations of the church. A lay person, who served on a committee to talk with several young clergy about his church's need for an associate pastor, observed that some of them seemed to view ministry as a "position" rather than as a "task." His comment is suggestive of the distinction between ordained ministry as a job and ordained ministry as servant leadership.

Servanthood is expressed in the Wesleyan tradition of ministry in the theological concepts of itineracy and appointment. Wesley's ideas about an itinerant and appointed ministry was articulated in American Methodism by Bishop Asbury, and his application of these principles became determinative for much of the nineteenth century. Although periodically there were challenges to episcopal authority, the dominant sentiment was that God's will was working in the church, and that the appointment system, with an itinerant ministry, was an effective means of ordering ministry for the urgent evangelical task. As late as the end of the nineteenth century, commentators would interpret appointment theologically in terms of God's will for the individual and the church. Describing the Methodist annual conference toward the end of the nineteenth century, A. B. Hyde wrote, "At first, the Bishop alone considered the men and field and made out the appointments. No preacher knew his destiny until the Bishop read the list at the close of the conference. The reading was usually taken as the speaking of Divine Providence and soon after the parting benediction the preachers, with strong heart and hope, were on their way to their new posts of service."[6] Perhaps the greatest significance of this historical observation is that it points to the conviction that the preachers interpreted their work as part of a grand plan which had ultimate significance. The deprivations and difficulties of the earthly life paled in comparison with the hopes and promises of the church triumphant.

Contemporary Methodism faces problems with itineracy and appointment. The institutional life of the church is more complex than it was even fifty years ago. Clergy couples and clergy spouses with careers complicate itineracy. Demands on the part of congregations for longer pastorates, and the complexities and costs of moves have reduced mobility. The introduction of mandatory consultation with pastor and people has changed Methodist polity dramatically. Perhaps the most significant impact on appointment and itineracy, however, is the development of a salary system in which the disparities between large, wealthy churches and small or poor churches are very great. Appointments are often based on salary considerations and years of service more than on the needs of the church and the particular gifts and graces of a pastor. We cannot use the Wesleyan theological understanding of an itinerant and appointed ministry, which is based on the missional needs of the church, in the face of a system that has developed in modern America along very different lines. The theology of appointment and itineracy requires a covenant collegiality which is the result of trust that appointment is based on the ultimate good of the whole church.

The ordained minister must early consider the question, "What constitutes success in ministry?" If success in ministry is thought to be a large church and a large salary, then one's life in ministry will always be unhappy, even if these things are achieved. Sometimes models of success in ministry are imported from other walks of life, the market model, the entertainment model, the management model, or the celebrity model. But when we borrow such models and apply them to ministry, we know it is not right. The only satisfactory model is that of Jesus himself. Whatever we mean by "success" in ministry, it can be measured only in relationship to the servant leadership of Christ. Such understanding leads us to say that, in spite of the enormous problems facing any system of ministerial deployment, and in spite of the perennial shortcomings of the institutional church, Christ has many services to be done, and the task of the ordained is to be servant leaders. Success in ministry may not be recognized by the church or the world; it is a gift of God, and is never the result of human calculation.

Teaching Authority

After the ordination prayer is finished and hands have been laid on an ordinand, his or her hands are placed on an open Bible as the bishop says, "Take thou authority as an elder in the Church to preach the Word of God, and to administer the holy Sacraments in the congregation."[7] Ordination takes place in the laying on of hands with prayer, and this statement follows to announce the authority ordination bestows. As we saw in our consideration of the history of ordination, ordination is tied to responsibility for church teaching.

John Wesley and early Methodism recognized the teaching role as central, and American Methodism received authoritative doctrinal guidelines from Wesley. These included his published sermons, his *Notes on the New Testament* (a biblical commentary), the *Minutes* of the English Methodist Conferences (in which doctrinal issues were articulated), and *The Sunday Service*, which included his revision of the Articles of Religion. Among Methodists these came to be known as the *Minutes*, the *Sermons*, the *Notes* and *The Sunday Service*.[8] These doctrinal materials were intended to maintain a vital link with the historic church, perpetuate Wesleyan emphases, and serve as guidelines for the three questions which constituted the earliest agenda for Wesley's conferences:

CHARACTER OF ORDAINED MINISTERS

1. What to teach? (the substance of the gospel)
2. How to teach? (the proclamation of the gospel)
3. What to do? (the gospel in action)

The answers to these questions were derived from conversation in conference. At first, conference consisted of Wesley and his preachers. In early American Methodism it was the bishops and ministers under appointment, but the bishops exercised strong control over doctrinal matters. They functioned as teachers to the church. After lay members were admitted to the annual conference representing charges, the conferences ceased to give much attention to doctrine, and Methodism has increasingly given less attention to the teaching office as the church has become more democratic. The attention given to teaching under Wesley and the early bishops gradually gave way to conferences which seldom deal with theological issues.

One of the major responsibilities of the ordained minister is the exercise of teaching authority, but it is one that has not been well understood recently. Today there is unwillingness to recognize teaching authority. The reluctance to recognize that the substance of faith proclamation matters is serious for the future of the church. Teaching authority requires knowledge of doctrine and thoughtful reflection on the way doctrine functions in pastoral ministry. Only so can the ordained minister guide the community in its effort to answer Wesley's three questions: What to teach? How to teach? What to do? Ordained ministers are servant leaders for the church on matters of theology and doctrine.

United Methodism will need to address the question of where, and by whom, its theological work should be done. A General Conference of perhaps a thousand delegates is no place for serious theological reflection. It may be that a standing theological commission should be established. Also the ordained clergy need to accept again their obligation for theological leadership. There are urgent theological questions facing the church which need attention from trained theologians in light of scripture interpreted by church tradition, Christian experience and faithful reason.

Authenticity and the Moral Life

The representative character of ordained ministers requires that attention be given to the moral life. The church has always expected that its clergy be morally exemplary, even though clergy have not always been so. The Methodist tradition, because of Wesley's concern for holiness, is particularly attentive to the moral lives of its ordained ministry. There are numerous aspects to be considered including such matters as how one thinks about "career," ministry and money, relationships with colleagues, human sexuality, marriage and family, health (diet, rest, exercise), leadership style, misplaced loyalty and compromise. Some of these have to do with ethics and etiquette, some with professional ethics, and some with the role of the ordained as examples of the Christian life.[9]

Periodically opposition will arise among clergy to the idea that they should be expected to be examples to the church. This argument is based on the observation that all Christians are ministers and therefore clergy should not have the added pressure of being morally exemplary. Certainly all Christians are called to ministry and the same standards are expected of all Christians. Ordained ministers, however, are "officially" representative figures to and of the church. This means that taking the yoke of obedience includes the representative role in total life. The ordained minister is not asked to lead a different moral life from lay Christians, but he or she is expected to live a life that is "officially" representative of the total ministry of the church.

A United Methodist ordained minister is obligated by vow to be able to justify all moral actions in terms of the way they reflect on the community being served and the way they teach the community about the Christian life. For example, traditionally Methodism included in the *Discipline* explicit prohibitions concerning the use of tobacco and beverage alcohol by clergy. Candidates were required to affirm they would abstain from both. In 1968 these specific prohibitions were removed, but in doing so the church called for "higher standards of self-discipline and habit formation in all personal and social relationships." It also demanded "dimensions of moral commitment that go far beyond any specific practices which might be listed."[10] Paragraph 404 states that all candidates for ordination must "agree to make a complete dedication of themselves to the highest ideals of the Christian life, and to this end agree to exercise responsible self-control, by personal habits conducive to bodily health, mental and emotional maturity, fidelity in marriage and celibacy in singleness, social responsibility, and growth in grace and the knowledge and love of God."[11] The standards are high because an authentic ministry requires commitment to live as a representative person. Seminaries need to give attention to their responsibility for aiding in the process of formation for clerical character. The way we shape our educational process, including the character of the persons teaching in seminaries, is of vital importance to the church's future.[12] The moral lives of ordained ministers are "officially" representative to and of the church; it "goes with the territory."

Ministry and the Yoke of Obedience

Franz Hildebrandt once observed that his reading of the New Testament convinced him that the picture of a minister of the gospel is not so much a person "in orders" as a person "under orders."[13] Hildebrandt was a good Methodist. As this book has suggested, Methodism's theology of ordination is concerned less with the matter of the validity of ministerial orders and more with the obligation of the ordained to be "under orders" for the gospel and church of Jesus Christ.

Being "under orders" means that one is obedient and accountable. Calvin insisted that one who is ordained must understand that "he is no longer a law unto himself, but bound in servitude to God and the church."[14] The language of service, bonds, orders, and obedience is not compatible with secular, liberal, twentieth-century America. We do not like to admit to any limitations of individual freedom. But the Christian gospel challenges us because we are confronted by Jesus himself who, "though he was in the form of God, did not count equality with God a thing to be grasped, but emptied himself, taking the form of a servant, being born in human likeness. And being found in human form he humbled himself and became obedient unto death, even death on a cross" (Phil. 2:6-8).

Ordained ministers are called to representative self-emptying lives of obedience and service. The greatest potential for renewal in ministry is for the ordained to reaffirm their high calling to live "under orders." Let John Wesley's prayer be our own:

> We take upon ourselves with joy the yoke of obedience. We are no longer our own, but thine. Put us to what thou wilt. Rank us with whom thou wilt. Put us to doing. Put us to suffering. Let us be employed for thee or laid aside for thee, exalted for thee or brought low for thee. Let us be full. Let us be empty. Let us have all things. Let us have nothing. We freely and heartily yield all things to thy pleasure and disposal.

NOTES

Introduction

1. Peter Taylor Forsyth, *The Church and the Sacraments* (London: Independent Press, 1917), p. 130.

Chapter 1

1. A recent study entitled "A Profile of Contemporary Seminarians" has just been completed by Ellis L. Larsen and James M. Shropshire. This study, which will be published in *Theological Education*, the journal of the Association of Theological Schools in the U.S. and Canada, is the source of the information in these two paragraphs.

2. Howard R. Bowen and Jack H. Schuster, *American Professors: A National Resource Imperiled* (New York: Oxford University Press, 1986). Among their studies is a fascinating report by the authors of the percentage of Phi Beta Kappa members in selected occupations, 1945-83. In 1945-49, 3.9 percent of persons elected to Phi Beta Kappa were in the ministry. They note a steady decline until in 1980-83 only 0.8 percent of persons elected were in the ministry.

3. *The Book of Discipline of the United Methodist Church* (Nashville: The United Methodist Publishing House, 1984), par. 404, footnote 3, p. 192.

4. See Albert C. Outler, *Theology in the Wesleyan Spirit* (Nashville: Tidings, 1975), pp. 20-22.

5. *The Works of John Wesley*, Oxford/ Bicentennial Edition, vol. 7, ed. Franz Hilderbrandt and Oliver A. Beckerlegge, "A Collection of Hymns for the Use of the People called Methodists" (Oxford: Oxford University Press, 1983), p. 644.

6. See Kenneth E. Rowe, "New Light on Early Methodist Theological Education," *Methodist History*, vol. 10, Oct., 1971, pp. 58-62.

NOTES

7. See Louis Dale Patterson, "The Ministerial Mind of American Methodism: The Courses of Study for the Ministry of the Methodist Episcopal Church, The Methodist Episcopal Church, South, and The Methodist Protestant Church." (Unpublished Ph.D. dissertation, Drew University, 1984).

8. See Roy A. Harrisville, *Ministry in Crisis: Changing Perspectives on Ordination and the Priesthood of All Believers* (Minneapolis: Augsburg, 1987).

9. See *The Priesthood of the Ordained Ministry* (London: Church House Publishing, 1986), pp. 87-90.

10. See Edward Schillebeeckx, *The Church With a Human Face: A New and Expanded Theology of Ministry* (New York: Crossroad, 1985).

11. *Baptism, Eucharist and Ministry*, Faith and Order Paper No. 111 (Geneva: World Council of Churches, 1982).

12. *The Book of Worship for Church and Home* (Nashville: The Methodist Publishing House, 1964), p. 387.

Chapter II

1. On the matter of Jesus' relationship to the Judaism of his day see E. P. Sanders, *Jesus and Judaism* (Philadelphia: Fortress Press, 1985). See especially pp. 116-119. In regard to the uniqueness of Jesus' ministry see James D.G. Dunn, *Unity and Diversity in the New Testament: An Inquiry into the Character of Earliest Christianity* (London: S.C.M. Press, 1977), pp. 105ff. To balance Dunn's emphasis, and to appreciate the community of Jesus' followers, see Gerd Theissen, *Sociology of Early Palestinian Christianity* (Philadelphia: Fortress Press, 1978), pp. 24-30.

2. See Luke 6:13-16. On this point see also E. P. Sanders, *Jesus and Judaism*, pp. 103-106.

3. See Mark 9:34-37; Luke 9:46-48.

4. Matt. 16:16.

5. Robert A. Spivey and D. Moody Smith, *Anatomy of the New Testament: A Guide to Its Structure and Meaning* (Third Edition. New York: MacMillan, 1982), p. 332.

6. See, for instance, 2 Cor. 3:6, 5:18; Eph. 4:1-7,11-16; Rom. 12:6-8; Col. 1:7,25, 4:7.

7. Max Weber provides important insight into the sociological role of charismatic ministries in the New Testament. See Max Weber, *The Sociology of Religion* (Boston: Beacon Press, 1963), pp. 60 ff, and p. 195. See also the discussion of Weber and Emil Durkheim on the idea of charisma in Talcott Parsons' "Introduction" to this edition, pp. xxxiii ff.

NOTES

8. See Gal. 3:28. In 1 Cor. 9:1 Paul asserts his own apostleship; and in Eph. 3:7-12 he discusses his commission which authorizes him to preach the gospel. See also 2 Cor. 3:6.

9. Dunn, p. 108.

10. Spivey and Smith, p. 134: "Luke-Acts was likely written sometime between A.D. 80 and 100."

11. See Acts 15.

12. See Acts 14:23 and Titus 1:5.

13. See James 5:14.

14. Wayne A. Meeks, *The First Urban Christians: The Social World of the Apostle Paul* (New Haven: Yale University Press, 1983), pp. 80-81.

15. Ibid., pp. 79-80.

16. See Dunn, pp. 121-123.

17. Eduard Schweizer, *Church Order in the New Testament* (Naperville, Ill.: Allenson, 1961).

18. Edward Schillebeeckx, *Ministry: Leadership in the Community of Jesus Christ* (New York: Crossroad: 1981), p. 9: "Thus originally the leaders of the community do not seem to have had any special name for their ministry ('those who labor among you, lead you and admonish you'). But the fact that there were local leaders in the communities even during the lifetime of the apostles, albeit ultimately under the oversight of the apostles, is historically undeniable."

19. For a helpful study of the problem of unity in the first century church see Paul J. Achtemeier, *The Quest for Unity in the New Testament Church* (Philadelphia: Fortress Press, 1987), See especially pp. 75-82.

20. Bernard Cooke, *Ministry to Word and Sacraments: History and Theology* (Philadelphia: Fortress Press, 1976), p. 63.

21. Joseph Blenkinsopp, *Celibacy, Ministry, Church* (London: Burns and Oates, 1969), p. 106.

22. Smyrneans 8:1-2.

23. Blenkinsopp emphasizes the fact that what later would be known as the monarchic episcopate is not evident in the New Testament. See p. 149.

24. For a collection of these documents and others on church, ministry and sacraments see Henry Bettenson, ed., *Documents of the Christian Church* (Oxford: Oxford University Press, 1963), pp. 62-79.

NOTES

25. The leadership of the early church and the reality of martyrdom is discussed by Christopher Dawson, *The Formation of Christendom* (New York: Sheed and Word, 1967), pp. 96 ff.

26. Ibid., p. 94.

27. One of the most useful histories of Christian ministry is H. Richard Niebuhr and Daniel Day Williams, eds., *The Ministry in Historical Perspectives* (New York: Harper and Row, 1956).

28. For a fuller treatment of the Christian theological roots of the development and meaning of the professions see my book *Doctors, Lawyers, Ministers: Christian Ethics in Professional Practice* (Nashville: Abingdon Press, 1982), especially pp. 17-30.

29. Roland H. Bainton, *The Reformation of the Sixteenth Century* (Boston: Beacon Press, 1952), see especially pp. 46-47. See also David C. Steinmetz, *Reformers in the Wings* (Philadelphia: Fortress Press, 1971) pp. 69-89.

30. "On the Ordering of the Divine Service in the Congregation," *D. Martin Luthers Werke*, vol. 4, (Briefwechsal: Weimar, 1930), p. 62.

31. *Institutes of the Christian Religion*, edited by John T. McNeill (Philadelphia: The Westminster Press, 1960), IV 3.12.

32. For a general history see A. G. Dickens, *The English Reformation* (New York: Schocken Books, 1964), or E. G. Rupp, *Studies in the Making of the English Protestant Tradition* (Cambridge: Cambridge University Press, 1965).

33. The phrase is from "The Order for Confirmation and Reception into the Church," *The Book of Worship for Church and Home*, (Nashville: The Methodist Publishing House, 1964), p. 12.

34. A helpful account of the relationship between the general and ordained ministries is provided by Norman Pittenger, *The Ministry of All Christians: A Theology of Lay Ministry* (Wilton, Connecticut: Morehouse - Barlow Co., 1983). "The chief concern, therefore, for both ordained and unordained, is that one's heart be pure - and this means, as the great Danish thinker Kierkegaard so vividly put it, that one 'wills one thing.' That 'one thing' is sacrifice and service" (emphasis mine), p. 11.

Chapter III

1. *The Works of John Wesley*, Bicentennial Edition, vol. 2, ed. Albert C. Outler (Nashville: Abingdon Press, 1985) Sermons II, "A Caution Against Bigotry," p. 70.

NOTES

2. For a thorough study of this period see Richard Heitzenrater's Introduction to *Diary of an Oxford Methodist: Benjamin Ingham, 1733-1734* (Durham: Duke University Press, 1985), pp. 1-47.

3. *The Works of John Wesley*, Oxford/Bicentennial Edition, vol. 25, ed. Frank Baker (Oxford: Oxford University Press, 1980), Letters I, "To the Revd. John Burton," p. 439.

4. *John Wesley's First Hymn-book: A Facsimile with Additional Material*, ed. Frank Baker and George Walton Williams (Charleston, S.C.: Dalcho Historical Society, and London: Wesley Historical Society, 1964).

5. *The Journal of the Rev. John Wesley, A.M.*, ed. Nehemiah Curnock (London: Epworth Press, 1938), vol. 1, p. 418.

6. *Journal*, vol. I, May 24, 1738, p. 476.

7. In his Introduction to his edited volume on John Wesley in the *Library of Protestant Thought*, Albert C. Outler uses the term minister "extraordinarius." See also the footnote in which he discusses Wesley's defense of his itinerant ministry in terms of his Oxford ordination. Albert C. Outler, ed., John Wesley (New York: Oxford University Press, 1964), p. 21.

8. *Works*, Oxford/Bicentennial Edition, vol. 25, ed. Frank Baker (Oxford: Oxford University Press, 1980) Letters I, "To James Hervey," p. 286.

9. *Works*, Oxford/Bicentennial Edition, vol. II, ed. Gerald R. Cragg (Oxford: Oxford University Press, 1980), "A Farther Appeal to Men of Reason and Religion," Part III, pp. 297-298.

10. *Works*, Bicentennial Edition, vol. 2, ed. Albert C. Outler (Nashville: Abingdon Press, 1985), Sermons II, "A Caution Against Bigotry," p. 74.

11. *Works*, Bicentennial Edition, vol. 3, Sermons III, "On Obedience to Pastors," p. 376.

12. Paul Chilcote, "John Wesley and the Women Preachers," (unpublished Ph.D. dissertation, Duke University, 1984). See also his book on this subject, *She Offered Them Christ* (Nashville: Abingdon Press, 1988).

13. Frank Baker comments on this in his book, *From Wesley to Asbury: Studies in Early American Methodism* (Durham: Duke University Press, 1976), p. 133.

14. *The Book of Worship of the Methodist Church* (Nashville: The Methodist Publishing House, 1964), p.387.

15. *Works*, Oxford/Bicentennial Edition, vol. 7, ed. Franz Hildebrandt and Oliver A. Beckerlegge (Oxford: Oxford University Press, 1983), "A Collection of Hymns for the Use of the People called Methodists," p. 694.

NOTES

16. See Geoffrey Wainwright, *The Ecumenical Moment: Crisis and Opportunity for the Church* (Grand Rapids: Eerdmans, 1983), pp. 189ff.

17. The standard scholarly study is Frank Baker, *John Wesley and the Church of England* (Nashville: Abingdon Press, 1970).

18. Wesley "...entirely repudiated the notion that Methodists were Dissenters." Rupert E. Davies, *Methodism* (London: Epworth Press, 1963), p. 99.

19. *The Letters of the Rev. John Wesley, A.M.*, ed. John Telford (London: The Epworth Press, 1931), vol. III, p. 182.

20. *Journal*, vol. III, p. 232, January 20, 1746.

21. *Letters*, vol. III, p. 182, To James Clark.

22. Colin W. Williams, *John Wesley's Theology Today* (Nashville, Abingdon Press, 1960), p. 225.

23. *Journal*, vol. VII, August 31, September 1, 1784, pp. 15-16, 23.

24. Ibid., September 2, 1784, p. 15.

25. *Letters*, vol. VII, p. 21.

26. Ibid., pp. 238-9.

27. A facsimile edition of *John Wesley's Sunday Service of the Methodists in North America*, with an introduction by James F. White, was published as a Methodist Bicentennial Commemorative Reprint in the Quarterly Review Reprint Series (Nashville: United Methodist Publishing House, 1984). All references are to this edition.

28. Albert C. Outler, "The Ordinal" in William F. Dunkle, Jr. and Joseph D. Quillian, Jr., eds., *Companion to the Book of Worship* (Nashville and New York: Abingdon Press, 1970), p. 113.

29. To his brother Charles, John wrote on August 19, 1785: "I firmly believe I am a scriptural episkopos as much as any man in England or in Europe." *Letters*, vol. 7, p. 284.

30. For an example of this argument see A.B. Lawson, *John Wesley and The Christian Ministry* (London: S.P.C.K., 1963), pp. 153-157. This excellent study shows all the serious problems with Wesley's ordinations according to Anglican theology. Albert Outler goes at this in a different way by downplaying the meaning of ordination for Wesley: "In his consistent usage, 'ordain' meant 'authorize,' no more, no less." Ibid.

NOTES

Chapter IV

1. John J. Tigert, *A Constitutional History of American Episcopal Methodism* (Nashville: Publishing House of the Methodist Episcopal Church, South, 1916), pp. 149 ff.

2. Thomas Ware, *Sketches of the Life and Travels of Rev. Thomas Ware, Written by Himself* (New York: Mason and Lane, 1839), p. 106.

3. For Bishop Asbury's interpretation of the events of the Christmas Conference and their meaning see *The Journal and Letters of Francis Asbury*, eds. J. Manning Potts, Elmer T. Clark, and Jacob S. Patton (London and New York: Epworth Press and Abingdon Press, 1958), vol. III, pp. 475-479. On the change of title see Tigert, pp. 240-241.

4. Tigert, p. 209. See also *The First Discipline and the Large Minutes* in Tigert, p. 549.

5. Ibid.

6. Ibid.

7. For a helpful discussion of Asbury's role in the shaping of Methodist worship in America see William Nash Wade, "A History of Public Worship in the Methodist Episcopal Church and Methodist Episcopal Church, South, From 1784 to 1905" (unpublished Ph.D. dissertation, University of Notre Dame, 1981), pp. 177-192.

8. *The Doctrines and Discipline of the Methodist Episcopal Church, South* (Nashville: The Methodist Episcopal Church, South Publishing House, 1926), paragraph 139.

9. *The Doctrines and Discipline of The Methodist Episcopal Church* (New York: Methodist Book Concern, 1924), paragraph 221.

10. *The Doctrines and Discipline of The Methodist Church* (New York and Nashville: The Methodist Publishing House, 1939), paragraph 287.

11. *Journal of the 1964 General Conference of The Methodist Church* (Nashville: The Methodist Publishing House, 1964), vol. I, pp. 392-405.

12. *The Book of Discipline of The United Methodist Church* (Nashville: The United Methodist Publishing House, 1968), paragraph 349.

13. *The Book of Discipline of The United Methodist Church* (Nashville: The United Methodist Publishing House, 1976), paragraph 408.

14. *The Book of Discipline of The United Methodist Church* (Nashville: The United Methodist Publishing House, 1984) paragraph 406.

NOTES

15. See, for instance, Timothy L. Smith, *Revivalism and Social Reform: American Protestantism on the Eve of the Civil War* (Nashville: Abingdon, 1957), p. 119: "The bishops expected every Methodist pastor to be an evangelist... The bishops themselves were aggressively evangelistic."

Chapter V

1. *The Book of Discipline of the United Methodist Church* (Nashville: The United Methodist Publishing House, 1984), paragraph 428, p. 216.

2. See 1 Timothy 3:1-13; Titus 1:5-9; 1 Peter 5:1-11.

3. This sentence has remained in subsequent editions of *The Disciplines*. In the 1984 edition it is found in paragraph 412, page 201.

4. Lisa Sowle Cahill nicely makes this point in her book *Between the Sexes: Foundations for a Christian Ethics of Sexuality* (Philadelphia: Fortress Press; New York: Paulist Press, 1985), p. 148: "Empirical evidence can be appropriated meaningfully in Christian ethics only if interpreted in the light of other, complementary sources: Scripture, tradition, and normative, as distinct from descriptive, accounts of the human."

5. *The Book of Discipline* (1984), paragraph 402, page 189.

Chapter VI

1. Peter Taylor Forsyth, *The Church and the Sacraments*. (London: Independent Press, 1917), p. 130.

2. See my article "The Ordained Ministry as a Profession: Theological Reflections on Identity," *Quarterly Review*, vol. 3, No. 2, pp. 21-20.

3. Robert K. Greenleaf, *Servant Leadership: A Journey into the Nature of Legitimate Power and Greatness*, (New York: Paulist Press, 1977). See especially pp. 7-48 and his chapter "Servant Leadership in Churches," pp. 218-248.

4. Tom Peters and Nancy Austin, *A Passion for Excellence: The Leadership Difference* (New York: Random House, 1985), p. xix.

5. Joseph Blenkinsopp, *Celibacy, Ministry, Church* (London: Burns and Oates, 1968), p. 185.

6. A. B. Hyde, *The Story of Methodism Throughout the World* (Philadelphia: P. W. Ziegler and Company, 1888), p. 416.

NOTES

7. *The Book of Worship for Church and Home*, (Nashville: The United Methodist Publishing House, 1964), p. 52. The alternate ordinal approved in 1980 puts it this way: "Faithfully exercise the authority given you by God and the Church to proclaim Good News in Word and Sacrament."

8. See Frank Baker, *From Wesley to Asbury* (Durham: Duke University Press, 1976), pp. 162-182.

9. A classic book in the field is Nolan B. Harmon, *Ministerial Ethics and Etiquette* (Nashville: Abingdon, 1987). Another useful book is Karen Lebacqz, *Professional Ethics: Power and Paradox* (Nashville: Abingdon, 1985).

10. *The Book of Discipline* (Nashville: The United Methodist Publishing House, 1984), p. 192.

11. Ibid.

12. For a very helpful articulation of these issues see Stanley Hauerwas, "Clerical Character: Reflecting on Ministerial Morality," *Word and World*, vol. VI, No. 2., pp. 181-193.

13. Franz Hildebrandt, "The Meaning of Ordination in Methodism," in Gerald O. McCulloh, ed., *The Ministry in the Methodist Heritage* (Nashville: Board of Education of The Methodist Church, 1960), p. 74.

14. *Institutes of the Christian Religion*, ed. John T. McNeill (Philadelphia: The Westminster Press, 1960), IV.3.16, p. 1067.

Bibliography

An Ordinal, The United Methodist Church: Adopted for Official Alternative Use by the 1980 General Conference. Nashville: The United Methodist Publishing House, 1979.

Asbury, Francis. *The Journal and Letters of Francis Asbury*. London: Epworth Press; Nashville: Abingdon Press, 1958.

Baker, Frank. *John Wesley and the Church of England*. Nashville: Abingdon, 1970.

_____. *From Wesley to Asbury*. Durham: Duke University Press, 1976.

_____. "Wesley's Ordinations," *Wesley Historical Society Proceedings*, XXIV 1944, pp. 76-103.

Baptism, Eucharist, and Ministry. Faith and Order Paper No. 111. Geneva, Switzerland: World Council of Churches, 1982.

Barnett, James Monroe. *The Diaconate: A Full and Equal Order*. New York: The Seabury Press, 1981.

Barrett, C. K. *The Signs of an Apostle*. (The Cato Lecture, 1969). London: Epworth Press, 1970.

Barnett, James Monroe. *The Diaconate: A Full and Equal Order*. New York: The Seabury Press, 1981.

Baxter, Richard. *The Reformed Pastor*. New York: T. Mason and G. Lane, 1837.

Blenkinsopp, Joseph. *Celibacy, Ministry, Church*. London: Burns and Oates, 1968.

Blizzard, Samuel W. *The Protestant Parish Minister: A Behavioral Science Interpretation*. Storrs, Conn.: Society for the Scientific Study of Religion, 1985.

Book of Discipline of the United Methodist Church. Nashville, Tennessee: United Methodist Publishing House, 1984.

BIBLIOGRAPHY

The Book of Worship for Church and Home. Nashville, Tennessee: The Methodist Publishing House, 1964, 1965.

Borgen, Ole. *John Wesley on the Sacraments*. Nashville: Abingdon, 1973.

Bowmer, John C. *Pastor and People: A Study of Church and Ministry in Wesleyan Methodism from the Death of John Wesley (1791) to the Death of Jabez Bunting (1858)*. London: Epworth Press, 1975.

_____. *The Sacrament of the Lord's Supper in Early Methodism*. Westminster: Dacre Press, 1951.

Brandon, Owen. *The Pastor and His Ministry*. London: S.P.C.K., 1972.

Brockman, Norbert, S.M. *Ordained to Service: A Theology of the Permanent Diaconate*. Smithtown, N.Y.: Exposition, 1980.

Brown, Raymond. *Priest and Bishop: Biblical Reflections*. New York: Paulist Press, 1970.

Brown, William Adams. *The Minister, His World and His Work*. Nashville, Tennessee: Cokesbury Press, 1937.

_____and May, Mark A. *The Education of American Ministers*. New York: Charles Scribner's Sons, 1934.

Cahill, Lisa Sowle. *Between the Sexes: Foundations for a Christian Ethics of Sexuality*. Philadelphia: Fortress Press, 1985.

Cameron, Richard M. *Methodism and Society in Historical Perspective*. New York and Nashville: Abingdon Press, 1961.

Campbell, Dennis M. *Doctors, Lawyers, Ministers: Christian Ethics in Professional Practice*. Nashville: Abingdon Press, 1982.

Campenhausen, Hans Freiherr von. *Ecclesiastical Authority and Spiritual Power in the Church of the First Three Centuries*. J.A. Baker, tr. Stanford, California: Stanford University Press, 1969.

Cannon, William Ragsdale. *The Theology of John Wesley*. New York and Nashville: Abingdon Press, 1946.

_____. "The Meaning of the Ministry in Methodism," *Methodist History*, 8:1 (October, 1969), 3-19.

Carroll, Jackson W. and Wilson, Robert L. *Too Many Pastors? The Clergy Job Market*. New York: Pilgrim Press, 1980.

_____. *Women of the Cloth: A New Opportunity for the Churches*. San Francisco: Harper & Row, 1981.

BIBLIOGRAPHY

Chiles, Robert E. *Theological Transition in American Methodism: 1790-1935*. New York and Nashville: Abingdon Press, 1965.

Congar, Yves. *Lay People in the Church*. London: Geoffrey Chapman, 1959.

Convocation of Methodist Theological Faculties, 1st, 1959. *The Ministry in the Methodist Heritage*, ed. Gerald O. McCulloh. Nashville, 1960.

Cooke, Bernard. *Ministry to Word and Sacraments: History and Theology*. Philadelphia: Fortress Press, 1976.

Cooke, Richard J. *History of the Ritual of the Methodist Episcopal Church*. Cincinnati: Jennings and Pye; New York: Eaton and Mains, 1900.

Davies, Rupert, and Rupp, Gordon, eds. *A History of The Methodist Church in Great Britain, Volume I*, London: Epworth Press, 1965.

Davies, Rupert E. *Methodism*. London: The Epworth Press, 1963.

Dearing, Trevor. *Wesleyan and Tractarian Worship: An Ecumenical Study*. London: Epworth Press and S.P.C.K., 1966.

Dickens, A. G. *The English Reformation*. New York: Schocken Books, 1969.

Dix, Gregory, ed. *The Treatise on the Apostolic Tradition of St. Hippolytus of Rome*. Reissued with corrections preface and bibliography by Henry Chadwick. London: S.P.C.K., 1968

_____. *The Question of Anglican Orders*. London: Dacre Press, 1948.

Dunn, James D. G. *Unity and Diversity in the New Testament: An Inquiry into the Character of Earliest Christianity*. London: S.C.M. Press, 1977.

Easton, B. S. "Jewish and Early Christian Ordination," *Anglican Theological Review*, V (1922-23), 308 ff. and VI (1923-24), 285 ff.

Ehrhardt, Arnold, *The Apostolic Ministry*. Edinburgh: Oliver and Boyd, 1958.

_____. *The Apostolic Succession in the First Two Centuries of the Church*. London: Lutterworth Press, 1953.

Elliott-Binns, L. *The Reformation in England*. Hamden, Connecticut: Archon Books, 1966.

Forsyth, Peter Taylor. *The Church and the Sacraments*. London: Independent Press, 1917.

George, A. Raymond. "Ordination," *A History of the Methodist Church in Great Britain*, ed. Rupert Davies. London: Epworth Press, 1978, vol. 2, pp. 143-160.

BIBLIOGRAPHY

_____. "Ordination in Methodism," *London Quarterly and Holborn Review*, 176 (April, 1951), 156-169.

Gerdes, Egon. *Informed Ministry: Theological Reflections on the Practice of Ministry in Methodism.* Zurich: Publishing House of the Methodist Church, 1976.

Greenleaf, Robert K. *Servant Leadership: A Journey into the Nature of Legitimate Power and Greatness.* New York: Paulist, 1977.

Greeves, Frederic. *Theology and the Cure of Souls.* London: Epworth, 1960.

Hale, Harry. *New Witnesses: United Methodist Clergywomen.* Nashville: Board of Higher Education and Ministry, 1980.

Hall, David. *The Faithful Shepherd: A History of the New England Ministry in the Seventeenth Century.* Chapel Hill: University of North Carolina Press, 1972.

Hanson, Anthony Tyrrell. *The Church of the Servant.* London: S.C.M., 1962.

_____. *Church, Sacraments and Ministry.* London: Mowbray, 1975.

_____. *The Pioneer Ministry: The Relation of Church and Ministry.* Philadelphia: Westminster, 1961.

Harmon, Nolan B. *The Rites and Ritual of Episcopal Methodism.* Nashville: Publishing House of the Methodist Episcopal Church, South, 1926.

Harrisville, Roy A. *Ministry in Crisis: Changing Perspectives on Ordination and the Priesthood of All Believers.* Minneapolis: Augsburg, 1987.

Harvey, A. E. *Priest or President?* London: S.P.C.K., 1975.

Hauerwas, Stanley. "Clerical Character: Reflecting on Ministerial Morality." *Word and World.* VI, 2, pp. 181-193.

Hawkins, Frank. "The Tradition of Ordination in the Second to the Time of Hippolytus." *The Study of Liturgy.* Edited by Cheslyn Jones, Geoffrey Wainwright, and Edward Yarnold. New York: Oxford University Press, 1978.

Herbert, George. *A Priest to the Temple, or Parson.* London: Methuen, 1899. London, S.P.C.K., 1961.

Holifield, E. Brooks. *The Gentlemen Theologians: American Theology in Southern Culture, 1795-1860.* Durham, N.C.: Duke University Press, 1978.

Holmes, Urban T., III. *The Future Shape of Ministry.* New York: Seabury Press, 1971.

BIBLIOGRAPHY

_____. *The Priest in Community: Exploring the Roots of Ministry*. New York: Seabury, 1978.

_____ and Robert E. Terwilliger, ed. *To Be a Priest*. New York: Seabury, 1975.

Holter, Don W. "Some Changes Related to the Ordained Ministry in the History of American Methodism," *Methodist History*, 13 (April, 1975), 177-194.

Hughes, Kent and Barbara. *Liberating Ministry from the Success Syndrome*. Wheaton, Illinois: Tyndale, 1987.

Hyde, A. B. *The Story of Methodism Throughout the World*. Philadelphia: P. W. Ziegler and Company, 1888.

Institute of Liturgical Studies. *Church and Ministry: Chosen Race, Royal Priesthood, Holy Nation, God's Own People*, ed. Daniel C. Brockopp. Valparaise, Indiana: Institute of Liturgical Studies, 1982.

Jenkins, Daniel. *The Protestant Ministry*. London: Faber and Faber, 1958.

Jewett, Paul K. *The Ordination of Women: An Essay on the Office of Christian Ministry*. Grand Rapids, Michigan: William B. Eerdmans, 1980.

Joint Lutheran/Roman Catholic Study Commission on the Gospel and the Church. *The Ministry in the Church*. Geneva: Lutheran World Federation, 1982.

Kelly, Robert L. *Theological Education in America*. New York: George H. Doran Company, 1924.

Kirkpatrick, Dow, ed. *The Doctrine of the Church*. New York and Nashville: Abingdon Press, 1964.

Kraemer, Hendrick. *A Theology of the Laity*. Philadelphia: Westminster Press, 1958.

Kung, Hans., ed. *The Plurality of Ministries*. New York: Herder and Herder, 1972.

_____. *Why Priests? A Proposal for a New Church Ministry*. Garden City, N.Y.: Doubleday 1972.

_____. *The Future of Ecumenism*. N.Y.: Paulist Press, 1969.

Langford, Thomas A. *Practical Divinity: Theology in the Wesleyan Tradition*. Nashville: Abingdon, 1984.

_____. *Wesleyan Theology: A Sourcebook* . Durham: Labyrinth Press, 1984.

BIBLIOGRAPHY

Lawson, A. B. *John Wesley and the Christian Ministry: The Sources and Development of His Opinions and Practices*. London: S.P.C.K., 1963.

Lawson, John. *Methodism and Catholicism*. London: S.P.C.K., 1954

Lincoln, C. Eric. *The Black Experience in Religion*. Garden City, N.Y.: Anchor Press, 1974.

Lynn, Kenneth S. *The Professions in America*. Boston: Beacon Press, 1963.

MacKie, Steven G. *Patterns of Ministry: Theological Education in a Changing World*. London: Collins, 1969.

Manson, T. W. *The Church's Ministry*. Philadelphia: Westminster Press, 1948.

Mathews, James K. *Set Apart to Serve: The Role of Episcopacy in the Wesleyan Tradition*. Nashville: Abingdon Press, 1985.

McBrien, Richard P. *Ministry: A Theological, Pastoral Handbook*. San Francisco: Harper and Row, 1987.

Mickle, Jeffrey P. "Toward a Revised Diaconate," *Quarterly Review*, II (1982), pp. 43-61.

Milner, Benjamin. *Calvin's Doctrine of the Church*. London: Brill, 1970.

Mitchell, Nathan. *Mission and Ministry: History and Theology in the Sacrament of Order*. Wilmington, Delaware: M. Glazier, 1982.

Moberly, R. C. *Ministerial Priesthood*. London: J. Murray, 1897.

Moede, Gerald F. *The Office of Bishop in Methodism: Its History and Development*. Zurich, Switzerland: Publishing House of The Methodist Church. New York and Nashville: Abingdon Press, 1964.

_____. *A Renewed Diaconate in The United Methodist Church?* Occasional Papers, Board of Higher Education and Ministry. Nashville: The United Methodist Publishing House, 1978.

Moule, C. F. D. "Deacons in the New Testament," *Theology*, LVIII, 1950, 405 ff.

Neely, Thomas B. *The Bishops and the Supervisional System of the Methodist Episcopal Church*. Cincinnati: Jennings and Graham, 1912.

Niebuhr, H. Richard. *The Purpose of the Church and its Ministry*. New York: Harper and Row, 1956.

_____ and Williams, Daniel Day, eds. *The Ministry in Historical Perspectives*. New York: Harper and Row, 1956.

BIBLIOGRAPHY

Neely, Thomas Benjamin. *The Evolution of Episcopacy and Organic Methodism*. New York: Phillips, 1888.

Norwood, Frederick A. *The Story of American Methodism: A History of the United Methodists and their Relations*. Nashville and New York: Abingdon Press, 1974.

Nouwen, Henri W. *Creative Ministry*. Garden City, New York: Doubleday, 1971.

_____. *The Living Reminder: Service and Prayer in Memory of Jesus Christ*. New York: Seabury Press, 1977.

_____. *The Wounded Healer: Ministry in Contemporary Society*. Garden City, New York: Doubleday, 1972.

Nygren, Herbert, "John Wesley's Changing Concept of the Ministry," *Religion in Life*, 31 (1962), 264-274.

Oden, Thomas C. *Pastoral Theology: Essentials of Ministry*. San Francisco: Harper and Row, 1983.

Outler, Albert C. *John Wesley*. New York: Oxford University Press, 1964.

_____. "The Ordinal." *Companion to The Book of Worship*. Nashville and New York: Abingdon Press, 1970.

_____. *Theology in the Wesleyan Spirit*. Nashville: Tidings, 1975.

Parrish, Carrie W. *The Journey of Women toward Ordination in the United Methodist Tradition: An Examination of the Efforts of Women*. North Carolina Conference, United Methodist Church, 1983.

Patterson, Louis Dale. "The Ministerial Mind of American Methodism: The Courses of Study for the Ministry of the MEC, MEC South, and MP." Unpublished Ph.D. dissertation, Drew University, 1984.

Pittenger, Norman. *The Ministry of All Christians: A Theology of Lay Ministry*. Wilton, Connecticut: Morehouse-Barlow, 1982.

Power, David N. *Ministers of Christ and His Church: The Theology of the Priesthood*. London: Geoffrey Chapman, 1969.

Pragman, James H. *Traditions of Ministry: A History of the Doctrine of the Ministry in Lutheran Theology*. St. Louis: Concordia, 1983.

Rattenbury, John Ernest. *The Eucharistic Hymns of John and Charles Wesley*. London: Epworth Press, 1948.

Richey, Russell E., "Evolving Patterns of Methodist Ministry," *Methodist History*, 22 (October, 1983), 25-37.

BIBLIOGRAPHY

_____. *Rethinking Methodist History; A Bicentennial Historical Consultation*. Nashville: Kingswood Books, United Methodist Publishing House, 1985.

Ruether, Rosemary, ed. *Women of Spirit: Female Leadership in the Jewish and Christian Traditions*. New York: Simon & Schuster, 1979.

Rupp, Gordon E. *Studies in the Making of the Protestant Tradition in the English Reformation*. London: Epworth Press, 1948.

Schaller, Lyle E., ed. *Women as Pastors*. Nashville: Abingdon, 1982.

Schillebeeckx, Edward. *Ministry: Leadership in the Community of Jesus Christ*. New York: Crossroad, 1981.

Schilling, S. Paul *Methodism and Society in Theological Perspective*. New York and Nashville: Abingdon Press, 1960.

Schweizer, Eduard. *Church Order in the New Testament*. Frank Clarke, tr. London. SCM Press, 1961.

Scott, Donald M. *From Office to Profession: The New England Ministry, 1750-1850*. Philadelphia: University of Pennsylvania Press, 1978.

Shelp, Earl E., ed. *The Pastor as Prophet*. New York: Pilgrim Press, 1985.

Shepherd, Massie. "The Development of the Early Ministry," *Anglican Theological Review* XXVI (1944)

Shockley, Grant, et. al. *Black Pastors and Churches in United Methodism*. Atlanta: Center for Research in Social Change, Emory University, 1976.

Simpson, Ervin P. Y. *Ordination and Christian Unity*. Valley Forge: Judson, 1966.

Spellman, Norman Woods. "The General Superintendency in American Methodism, 1784-1870." Yale Dissertation, Ann Arbor, Michigan: University Microfilms, 1973.

Steinmetz, David C., "Asbury's Doctrine of Ministry," *Duke Divinity School Review*, 40 (Winter, 1975), 10-17.

Tavard, George H. A *Theology for Ministry*. Wilmington, Delware: Michael Glazier, 1983.

Thompson, Edgar W. *Wesley: Apostolic Man: Some Reflections on Wesley's Consecration of Dr. Thomas Coke*. London: Epworth Press, 1957

Thurian, Max. *Priesthood and Ministry: Ecumenical Research*. London: Mowbray, 1983.

BIBLIOGRAPHY

Tigert, John J. *A Constitutional History of American Episcopal Methodism*. Nashville: Publishing House of the Methodist Episcopal Church, South, 1916.

Tuell, Jack M. *The Organization of the United Methodist Church*. Nashville: Abingdon, 1977.

Vos, Wiebe, and Wainwright, Geoffrey. *Ordination Rites: Papers Read at the 1979 Congress of Societas Liturgica*. Rotterdam: The Liturgical Ecumenical Center Trust, 1980.

Wagoner, Walter D. *Bachelor of Divinity*. New York: Association Press, 1963.

Wainwright, Geoffrey. *The Ecumenical Movement: Crisis and Opportunity for the Church*. Grand Rapids: William B. Eerdmans, 1983.

Weidman, Judy, ed. *Women Ministers*. San Francisco: Harper & Row, 1981.

Wesley, John. *The Journal of John Wesley*. Edited by Nehemiah Curnock. Standard edition. London: The Epworth Press, 1938.

_____. *The Letters of John Wesley*. Edited by John Telford. Standard edition. London: The Epworth Press, 1938.

_____. *The Works of John Wesley*. Edited by Thomas Jackson. 3rd ed. London: John Mason, 1829. Grand Rapids, Michigan: Baker Book House, 1978.

_____. *The Works of John Wesley*. Edited by Frank Baker. Oxford/Bicentennial Edition. Oxford: Oxford University Press and Nashville: Abingdon Press. [Individual volumes, which carry various publication dates, are listed in the end notes.]

What Is Ordination Coming To? Report of a Consultation on the Ordination of Women . . . September, 1970, ed. Brigalia Bam. Geneva: World Council of Churches, 1971.

Williams, Colin W. *John Wesley's Theology Today*. New York and Nashville, Abingdon Press, 1960.

DATE DUE